Leading to Change the World

From Housekeeper to Director to Doctor

Leading to Change the World

One Black Woman's Journey to Positions of Leadership in Predominantly White Institutions

Leslye Renee Kornegay, EdD

Internet addresses given in this book were accurate at the time it went to press.

Cover design by Makayla Perry
Cover photo by Simone Robertson

Printed in the United States of America
Published in Hellertown, PA
Library of Congress Control Number 2024914347
ISBN 979-8-89420-005-7

For more information or to place bulk orders, contact the author or the publisher at Jennifer@BrightCommunications.net.

Bright
COMMUNICATIONS

I dedicate this and credit the inspiration for my lifelong pursuit of knowledge to my parents. To my mother that is no longer physically present, you planted those seeds of hope when I was born. You gave me the courage to become the woman I am today. Through your constant love, prayers, and support, I have been able to navigate the challenges in my life. To my step-father, your hard work as the provider of our family served as a model for me as I grew into adulthood. To my father, while you are no longer physically present, I thank you for my childhood memories. They say a child picks its parents; if that is true, then I have been truly blessed because each of you have helped to shape the woman that I have become today. I am eternally grateful to be your daughter.

I also dedicate this to my sister, who has always been a source of strength to me.

Contents

You can ban a book
Try to redact history
Move the finishing lines
Attempt to belittle
Our womanhood
And paint your self with hate
But we still win
We are
Undefeated
With
Uncommon favor
From
An Unbelievable God!
by Leslé Honoré

Author's Note

This manuscript was originally published in 2012 as the author's Scholarly Personal Narrative (SPN) that was the cumulation of her doctoral studies. It has been updated and adapted into book form for all readers. The author currently works at Duke University as the Executive Director for Facilities-UEVS. Her career in facilities management has spanned over 35 years. Additionally, she has served in a faculty role for the past 14 years and has founded a nonprofit organization, the Kornegay Foundation. She can be reached at kornegayfoundation@gmail.com or KornegayKonsulting@gmail.com.

Chapter One: Herstorical Background

This Is Who I AM

Racial Identity

I was born in February of 1959. My race was marked as "Negro" on my birth certificate. Sara and Joseph Kornegay, Sr. welcomed me into the world on a gorgeous sunny day on HOMEstead Air Force Base in Miami, Florida. Two years later, the youngest couple to ever reside in the White House became the President and First Lady of the United States. The Kennedys ushered in what has become known as the Camelot era, which has been described as one of our nation's most romantic periods, as the Kennedys were the closest thing to royalty the White House had seen.

My birth certificate is a constant reminder of my heritage. My ancestors, at least some of them, are descendants of African slaves who were stolen from their HOMEland and trafficked across the Atlantic. The word "Negro" also serves as a continued reminder of the struggles and sacrifices endured by my enslaved ancestors. Thanks to the civil rights movement, the word "Negro" was no longer used on birth certificates to identify race after 1964; it was replaced with "African American" and, later, with "Black." As a young adult, I learned that I could replace the "Negro" on my birth certificate with "African American" or "Black" if I wanted to. However, I chose not to change it. I believed then, as I do now, that you cannot erase the past by simply replacing one word with another.

Political

At the time of this writing, it has been 70 years since the landmark decision of *Brown vs. Board of Education* was passed into law, calling for integration in our public schools and ending racial segregation. It has been 60 years since the Civil Rights Bill was enacted into law and about 64 years since the onset of the second wave of the women's rights movement. In my lifetime, I have witnessed many of the dreams that Martin Luther King Jr. wrote about in his famous "I Have a Dream" speech come true.[1] King envisioned a world where one day all children, regardless of their color, would be able to attend the same schools and where all people would have the same access to public facilities. While the civil rights movement did improve the quality of life for many Black people, the old Negro anthem, "We Shall Overcome," has not been fully realized.[2] The social, historical, and political context surrounding the period of history that I was born into greatly impacted my personal and professional development as a Black woman and leader.

Social Identity

In September of 2011, ABC News aired a special revealing audiotape recordings of Jacqueline Kennedy that had been sealed for nearly 50 years. The tapes were made after the assassination of President Kennedy in 1963. Caroline Kennedy, the surviving daughter of President John F. Kennedy (JFK) and Jacqueline Kennedy, gave an interview and explained why she had decided it was time to finally release the audiotape recordings to the public. During the interview, Caroline shared how she had struggled over the years with whether or not to release the recordings because many of the comments her mother made were resonant of another time in our history. The recordings revealed the thoughts of a young Jacqueline Kennedy who was nothing like the woman she would ultimately become years later.

My mother and I watched the special together, and we reflected on the reality of what life was like for women during that era. I wondered if the First Lady might have felt that it was not "her place" to do certain things, like publicly display affection for her husband or voice her own opinions. It seemed to me that she relied completely on her husband's thoughts and actions; whatever they were, they had to be right. She even suggested that Martin Luther King Jr. had to have been "tricky" because JFK had said so. Mrs. Kennedy also noted that she believed it was her responsibility to have a calm environment for her husband when he came HOME because he had stressful days at work.

My mother reminded me that women were considered second class citizens during those days—even more so than we are now. They could not own property, they were considered "old maids" if they were not engaged to marry before the age of 18, and it was not acceptable for women to live alone or to date men without a chaperone. Women were not really allowed to have an identity separate from their husbands. There were even handbooks and marriage pamphlets describing how to be the ideal woman for your husband.[3] There were strict rules about how they were allowed to behave, like the mandate that women were not to be seen smoking in public. Education beyond high school was only to obtain a social skill, not to pursue a career. Society also dictated what women could wear, down to the hemline of their dresses and skirts. Pants were not to be worn by women in public. Men wore the pants—literally and figuratively—and women were groomed to take care of the HOME, the husband, and the children. Nothing more. Black women who were leaders outside of their families during this time did so at a risk to themselves. Access into Predominantly White Institutions (PWIs) of higher learning did not occur for Black women until after the 1960s.[4]

The Jacqueline Kennedy interviews left me with an appreciation for how much progress women have made in our society over the past 50-plus years.

If white American feminist theory need not deal with the difference between us, and the resulting difference in our oppressions, then how do you deal with the fact that the women who clean your houses and tend your children while you attended conferences on feminist theory are, for the most part, poor women and women of Color? What is the theory behind racist feminism?[5]

A number of Black scholars have noted that Black women have always worked outside the household and often in domestic roles to support White women and White households.[6] Many scholars have also described what is known as the first wave of the feminist movement as a White women's movement.[7] White women's feminism focused on equalizing their stance with White men.[8] Since Black women at that time did not have equal footing with White males or White women, the first women's movement was not a movement for all women.[9] As cited in Angela Humphrey Brown,

> The relative significance of race, sex, or class in determining the conditions of Black women's lives is neither fixed nor absolute but, rather, is dependent on the socio-historic context and the social phenomenon under consideration. African American scholars as well as some EuroAmerican scholars have suggested that White women have benefited greatly from their position.[10]

Additionally, Peggy Macintosh as cited in Brown suggested,

> White women have been oppressed; they have also had privileges that come with being White in America. Conversely, as a result of their positionality, African American women have not had the same opportunities as their White female counterparts. Moreover, while African American men have suffered reality, the unit of analysis around race, generally speaking, includes their

voice, while often silencing or omitting the voices of African American women. Hence, some Euro-American feminists and some African American scholars have suggested that African American women live with the double-jeopardy of racial and gender oppression. The double-jeopardy African American women encounter in terms of race and sex is viewed by some feminists as a reason for conduction research especially on Black women and their role and contributions to American society.[11]

Charisse Jones and Kumea Shorter-Goodsen, authors of the book *Shifting: The Double Lives of Black Women in America,* coined the phrase "shifting" to describe a common theme that grew out of their "Voices Project" study on Black women in America.[12] Their research found that "in response to this relentless oppression Black women in our country have had to perfect what they called 'shifting,' a sort of subterfuge that African Americans have long practiced to ensure their survival in our society."[13] Throughout history, Black women have been oppressed and marginalized by White men, White women, and Black men.[14] Black women have also always been the backbone of the families they have participated in.

We sired the master's children, we breastfed the mistresses' offspring, we cooked and cleaned for the master and his family, yet our value was less than the family mule.[15]

Sojourner Truth was one of those strong Black women who advocated for enslaved women. Truth was a Black abolitionist woman, and she wrote a now famous letter to the 18th century White society and asked the question, "Ain't I a woman too?"[16]

"Wall, chilern, whar dar is so much racket dar must be somethin' out o' kilter. I tink dat 'twixt de niggers of de Souf and de womin at de Norf, all talkin' 'bout rights, de white men will be in a fix pretty soon. But what's all dis here talkin' 'bout?

"Dat man ober dar say dat womin needs to be helped into carriages, and lifted ober ditches, and to hab de best place everywhar. Nobody eber helps me into carriages, or ober mud-puddles, or gibs me any best place! And a'n't I a woman? Look at me! Look at my arm! I have ploughed, and planted, and gathered into barns, and no man could head me! And a'n't I a woman? I could work as much and eat as much as a man—when I could get it—and bear de lash as well! And a'n't, I a woman? I have borne thirteen chilern, and seen 'em mos' all sold off to slavery, and when I cried out with my mother's grief, none but Jesus heard me! And a'n't I a woman? "Den dey talks 'bout dis ting in de head; what dis dey call it? What's dat got to do wid womin's rights or nigger's rights? If my cup won't hold but a pint, and yourn holds a quart, wouldn't ye be mean not to let me have my little half-measure full? Den dat little man in black dar, he say women can't have as much rights as men, 'cause Christ wan't a woman! Whar did your Christ come from? Whar did your Christ come from? From God and a woman! Man had nothin' to do wid Him."

As our country entered into the Camelot era, 100 years after Truth's question was posed, Black women were still fourth-class citizens (White men, White women, Black men and, lastly, Black women), cleaning, cooking, and caring for White families.[17] According to my mother, none of the women in our family ever did domestic work for anyone outside of their own families. I am the only one in my family who made housekeeping a profession. Novels like The Color Purple[18] and The Help[19] really helped me to visualize what life must have been like for Black women during the 1960s. According to Jones and Shorter-Goodsen,

> The ways in which a Black woman shifts have of course changed over time. An enslaved woman or a Black woman living under the hell of Jim Crow would have to shift literally, casting her eyes down when a white passenger came into view, moving her body off a sidewalk or to the back of a crowded bus when a white passenger came into view. Today, shifting is more subtle and insidious—keeping silent

when a white colleague sexually harasses her, for fear she will not be believed; acting eager but not aggressive at work, so as not to alienate a white boss; and then shifting again at HOME to appease a Black man who himself has to live with the pain and unfairness of society's prejudice and hate. Perhaps more than any other group of Americans, Black women are relentlessly pushed to serve and satisfy others and made to hide their true selves to placate White Colleagues, Black men, and other segments of the community. They shift to accommodate differences in class as well as gender and ethnicity.[20]

When my mother and I talked about the Jacqueline Kennedy tapes, she shared with me that she never felt oppressed during the civil rights and women's rights movements. She always felt she could do whatever she wanted to do. In fact, my grandmother used to tell her that she was afraid for her sometimes because my mother would say whatever she felt like saying and my grandmother was afraid that one day somebody might hurt my mother. My mother's philosophy about life and the way that she raised me truly embraced the womanist movement as opposed to the feminism and Black Feminism movements.

While I was born during this time in history, my mother shielded me from many of the -isms (race, sex, gender, and class) while I was growing up. In my opinion, I did not personally experience racism, sexism, genderism, or classism until after I entered the workforce as an adult. I attributed this to being raised in the military (which was integrated) and living in military institutions (traveling domestically and globally) until I was 13 years old (returning to the United States in 1972 after the civil rights bill was enacted and the Black power and women's movements were in full swing). Therefore, my experiences as a Black child were uniquely different from many Black children's during this time. As cited in Patricia Hill Collins, "The concept of Womanist, which was first coined by Alice Walker, a term she described as 'womanist is to feminist as purple is to lavender,' addressed the notion of the solidarity of humanity."[21] Hill Collins suggested.

to Walker, "one is a 'womanist' when one is 'committed to the survival and wholeness of entire people, male and female.' A womanist is 'not a separatist, except periodically for health' and is 'traditionally universalist, as is "Mama, why are we brown, pink, and yellow, and our cousins are white, beige, and black?" Ans: Well you know the colored race is just like a flower garden, with every color flower represented."(1983, xi)[22]

Collins suggested that by redefining all people as "people of color," Walker universalizes what are typically seen as individual struggles while simultaneously allowing space for autonomous movement of self-determination.[23]

My mother is largely responsible for shaping the person that I have become today. Although there are a number of women in my life who I have admired and respected, my mother was my first role model, through her daily struggles as a working mom. She is my *Shero* and has been a pillar of strength for me throughout my life. My mother was always a leader and very vocal. She had confidence in herself and her first-born daughter.

After I was born, when the time came to name me, my father wanted to give me his middle name, Leslie. My mother agreed, but on her own terms. She decided to spell my name LESLYE (Lez-Sel-Lee), a spelling that was considered risqué at the time. Fifty-two years later, I still have never met anyone who spells their name like mine. Even then, my mother wanted to be sure I would have my own identity.

My name was one of many seeds my mother planted for her first-born girl. She lovingly watered, weeded, and tended her garden with all of the loving care she could, and as I grew into womanhood, the seeds she planted (courage, finding my place/outsider, resilience) bloomed into the promise of one Black mother's many sacrifices for her child to have the opportunities to experience a life she never had. My mother set the stage for me to challenge the status quo, to be able to face what life had to offer with courage before I even uttered my first words.

I am a first-generation college student—the only one of my mother's three children and one step-child to receive all three degrees: an undergraduate, graduate, and doctorate degree. In my professional life, I have had many firsts. I was the first Black woman to hold the position of Deputy Assistant Director, a senior leadership position in the facilities department at a major higher education Predominately White Institution(PWI) in a State University system, as well as the first Black woman to hold the positions of Associate Director of Housing Facilities and Operations at a major higher education PWI in Massachusetts, and Director of Custodial Services at the University of Vermont (UVM).

While I have had many firsts, my trajectory from housekeeper to director to Doctor of Education has taken an unusual path into leadership. I never envisioned myself as a role model for women like myself, but my personal narrative is full of stories encompassing my vision to find my purpose in life. While I had informal role models in my personal life, I never had formal mentors to emulate the kind of courageous leader that I have become. As you can imagine, it was a real surprise for me to learn from my peers and my supervisor that I am perceived as a role model and that others could learn from my experiences.

When I finally decided on the topic for my dissertation, I recall what my advisor, Robert Nash, the leading scholar of Scholarly Personal Narrative (SPN)—to be defined later in the Methodology section—said to me. He commented that my SPN would be unique because to his knowledge no one like me had done an SPN before in my research area. When I reflect upon my early adult years, many of the professions that are accessible to women like me today either did not exist or were not accessible to marginalized groups. While society has become more tolerant and accepting with the array of racial and gender differences in the workplace, the population in public higher educational institutions continues to reflect a small portion of Black women in executive leadership positions on predominantly White campuses.

My journey from housekeeper to director to Doctor of Education spanned a career of more than 35 years at PWIs. My personal and professional story is filled with the challenges and barriers, obstacles and opportunities I have encountered in a profession and institutions that were underrepresented by Black women in executive leadership roles. My journey from an entry level position, to midlevel, and eventually to executive management includes the completion of two post-secondary degrees and a doctoral degree, as well as numerous promotions, various transformations in leadership styles, and several relocations.

As a doctoral student in the Leadership and Policy Studies Program at UVM, I was able to align my experiences as a Black woman in an executive leadership position with my coursework throughout the program. Very early in my search for a dissertation topic, I wanted to better understand how Black women in executive leadership roles lead their organizations. More specifically, how was their leadership formed? Who were their role models? Who taught them to lead? Did their leadership trajectory take a normative path similar to my own? What strategies have they used to sustain their leadership? My interest was in these women's stories and whether their experiences were similar to my own. After spending a year exploring which writing methodology would enable me to include my marginalized voice into my research topic, I came to the realization it was not an option for me to exclude myself from my own work. Therefore, I decided to utilize SPN to share my story.

During the pre-search phase of my dissertation journey, I quickly ascertained from the existing literature on my topic of interest that the life experiences and stories of others did not reflect my unique life experience as a Black woman. Early in the literature research, I exposed myself to existing SPNs that, at first glance, paralleled my journey in higher education. A more thorough review of these resources revealed some of the stories were told through the experiences, perspectives, and interpretations of Black and Chicano men.[24] It should be noted that the social, historical, and political context that impacted their journeys also affected my journey 20 years later. Some of the pre-search I explored came from SPN writers such as Jacob Diaz, Alvin Sturdivant, and DeMethra Bradley, which highlighted parts of my experience.

In his SPN dissertation, Jacob Diaz suggested, "Experiences can offer knowledge to the society about the intricate relationship between power structures, self, and theory."[25] Diaz's personal experience of feeling like an outsider as a young Chicano male began in elementary school and was replicated in middle school, high school, and college.[26] Being a member of two marginalized populations, Black and female, I have often felt that I did not have a place in the personal and professional world because my experiences stemmed from the political, social, and historical climate of the time, as a result of being born in the United States before 1960. Some of my elementary school experiences were very different from Diaz's and the other stories because I was exposed to both segregated and integrated schools.

Interestingly, Patricia Hill Collins described this outsider feeling as "outsider within." She suggested that this is not an uncommon feeling among Black women and that it has been experienced throughout Black history by slaves and later freed slaves who worked in domestic roles such a childcare and housekeeping for White households.[27] Additionally, Diaz's story was told through the perspective of a Chicano man while Alvin Sturdivant's story was told through the perspective of a Black man.

Finally, DeMethra Bradley's journey described her experience as a second-generation college student whose mother was first-generation. This was unlike my story, as I am a first-generation college student and the only one of my mother's children to obtain a college degree in general.[28] While Bradley and I both identify as Black women, a key difference in our stories is that Bradley's mother attended college, and my mother holds only a high school diploma. When it comes to the doctoral journey, Juliana Mosley summed it up very nicely in her story regarding attaining her doctoral degree in a predominantly White public institution, *Just Do It.*[29]

Another author whose story resonated with my own was Sherryl Weston. She shared her story in the book *Our Stories II: The Experiences of Black Professionals on Predominantly White Campuses.* In her story, she talked about some of the issues that influenced her childhood, which she believed contributed to her overall development as an administrator working in a PWI. I found many common themes to Sherryl's story and my own. One example is we both grew up in the military. We both experienced constant relocations throughout our childhood. As a result, we both learned to adapt to various changes due to the exposure of constant change in our lives at an early age.[30] Additionally, I discovered that we both lacked formal and informal mentors in our lives. We also both believed some of the mistakes and choices that were made in our careers navigating the obstacles and challenges in PWIs could have been avoided if formal mentors had been present throughout our lives.[31]

All of these stories are important because they helped me to acknowledge very early in my pre-search stage that my personal and professional experiences are unique to the literature and that my experiences need to be front and center in my research. It is because of the lived experiences through stories, biographies, autobiographies, personal narratives, and SPN writings that I am able to find some commonality in the literature with my own personal and professional journey.

My goal in this book is to shed light on my unique story as a Black woman in executive leadership positions and my journey from housekeeper to director to Doctor of Education. Through these chapters, I will explore the major themes central to my experiences of leading with moral courage, including my *SHEROs*, place/outsider, moral courage, journey, adversity, transformation, and adapting in two worlds. Within each theme, I will explore my experiences from a broader perspective, utilizing research and other writings to shed light on my own narrative. While there is evidence of a growing body of literature on women and Black women in higher education leadership roles, what is missing for me in the literature are stories that are unique to my life experiences.[32] Therefore, I will draw upon various biographies, literature, and personal communications in order to universalize my own experience.

I will also reflect on my earlier SPN "Leading with Moral Courage at a Research I, Public Ivy University: An African

American Woman's Journey from Custodian, to Custodial Director, to Doctoral Student,"[33] which only touched on a tip of the iceberg that is my entire journey. There is much more to my story, and writing my first SPN made me realize that I wanted the "mesearch" of my research to be much deeper. Additionally, the cohort of Black women in executive leadership roles within higher education is a very small group (8.1 percent).[34] Typically in a qualitative and quantitative research design, there is an expectation to assure the anonymity of the participants involved in the study. This can be difficult to do in a PWI like UVM. A recent example is a qualitative research project I completed on moral and ethical leadership for one of my doctoral courses.[35] Originally, I wanted to interview Black women in senior executive roles. However, due to the scarcity of women in this population on UVM's campus—I was one of four Black women in executive positions at the time—I decided to expand my topic to women in general, which included one Black woman in this group. Going beyond the UVM community for participants was not an option for me at the time.

Because my research is about who I am and what I do, and I am among the population that I am interested in learning more about, I believe my story would help to fill the void in the existing literature.

In summary, while I have had many firsts, my trajectory from housekeeper to director to Doctor of Education has taken an unusual path into leadership. I never envisioned myself as a role model for women similar to me; my personal narrative is full of stories of my vision quest to find my purpose in life. While I had informal role models in my personal life, I never had formal role models to emulate the kind of courageous leader that I have become in my professional life.

When I reflect upon my early adult years, many of the professions that are accessible for women like myself today either did not exist or were not accessible to marginalized groups. Although society has evolved into a more tolerant acceptance of racial and gender diversity in the workplace, my experience in higher education PWIs continues to have a small population of Black women in executive leadership.

I believe through the use of SPN methodology, this book will bring into focus an invisible population in higher education senior administration. Through SPN, the voice of one of the most marginalized groups in our society, Black women, can be shared. Through sharing my stories, I can contribute to the growing body of research on Black women in higher education.

Finally, I can draw upon my own personal and professional narratives to expound upon the universal themes that helped shape my leadership transformation from a housekeeper to director to Doctor of Education and bridge the "so what?" and "now what?" of my research as it relates to other Black women in the future.[36] I hope that the lessons that I have amassed in my lifetime can apply to senior leaders or people who aspire to become one.

Finally, this book will share my unique experiences throughout my journey and the strategies that I have used to sustain my leadership. It was my intent that my dissertation would expand upon my unique experiences leading in PWIs, including reflections and interpretations of my experiences, and I intend to continue that work here. Throughout this book, I will keep the element of universality the major focus of my narrative. Overall, my goal will be for others to read my story, hear my voice, perhaps find themselves in my narrative, and know that their marginalized voices can be heard as well.

In the following chapters, I will start by sharing my personal and professional journey, using my own narrative and the pivotal moments on my journey and how I developed and sustained my leadership. I will explore how my leadership was formed and how I have struggled at times in my journey into leadership as a Black woman working in PWIs. Through the incorporation of the narratives of scholars and educators, I will illustrate the personal journeys and lessons learned. I will examine the research genre of SPN and explain why I selected SPN for my dissertation. I will explore the importance of narratives and how they are embraced throughout African American culture as a way of teaching and learning about our differences. Through the exploration of the social, historical, and political context that I was born into, I will examine the impact of navigating challenging *"-ism"* dynamics from my personal and professional experiences and incorporate the stories of others through the lenses of leadership, social capital, Black Feminism, and Womanism.

Additionally, I will uncover challenging racial, sexual, gender, class, and hostile environment dynamics within my personal and professional experiences within PWIs. By incorporating personal stories and the stories of others, I will explore effective coping strategies for Black women leading in PWIs to sustain their leadership. I will discuss the importance of my leadership role working with marginalized populations in the workforce. Through the utilization of SPN methodology, I will write letters to SPN Methodology, my mother, my father, myself, Black women in Higher Education Leadership, and finally a letter to PWIs. I will examine how I made meaning through experiences with racism, sexism, genderism, and classism within hostile environments and examine how others make meaning of their experiences.

Chapter Two:
SPN Methodology

Narrative has also become essential to understanding the social, emotional, and physical conditions of populations that have been, and some would argue continually are, left out of mainstream research.[37]

An SPN (scholarly personal narrative) research design, which is when the author puts herself in her research, telling her story, is the best way for me to share my personal and professional narrative as a Black woman in executive leadership. As I shared earlier, throughout my doctoral coursework, I often injected my personal experiences into my research and writing. It was not until I was exposed to SPN that I was able to truly include my marginalized voice in my research. Writing my earlier SPN paper gave me a license to tell my story in my own voice, using a writing style that did not require me dressing my paper up for the peer-reviewed process commonly found in qualitative and quantitative research papers using American Psychological Association (APA) formatting. While other research methodologies have their value in the research field, I believe the best way for me to unleash my voice is through SPN. My professional experiences cannot be told without including my personal narrative. Only by sharing our most personal experiences can we begin to unmask the obstacles, barriers, and challenges that (Black) women have experienced in order to effect social change. I believe my story is one that many (Black) women will be able to identify with, and perhaps they can also take some of the lessons learned from my narrative to effect social change in their own lives.

Narrative has its origins in a number of the social and humanities disciplines, including education. In this methodology, the researcher studies one or more individuals, focuses on their stories, reports the data (e.g., themes that emerge from the participants' narratives), and then often includes the relational meaning of those experiences in their research. There have been a variety of forms found in narrative research, including biographical study, autobiographical study, life history, and oral history.[38] In these research designs, the researcher focuses on understanding the causes and effects of events reported via personal reflections from the participants being studied.[39] Narrative research has served a number of functions, including understanding the social transmission of experience such as parables, proverbs, moral and mystic tales, and the passing on of cultural heritage or organizational culture; to persuade or give credibility to something; and to help groups define an issue or their collective stance toward an issue. The narratives of several become a common experience.[40] What distinguishes SPN from other forms of narrative inquiry is that the writer is not bound to any set order (placing personal history into any chronological order), and the personal narrative and themes are grounded in scholarly research that has universal implications for a group(s).[41]

Nash and Bradley suggest that an "autoethnographer is primarily interested in examining the cultural and contextual influences on a writer's self-reflection. An autoethnographer's top priority is to apply, in a rigorous way, an ethnographic, interview type, cultural methodology to the study of the self."[42] They go on to state that, "By using the scientifically established anthropological method of studying one's life within the context of one's culture, the auto ethnographer is able to avoid being excessively preoccupied with the self, as well as overdoing the telling of personal stories and drawing on memories that might be self-serving and contrived."[43] Autoethnography, by its very nature, would limit the very essence of what an SPN should be about, which is to share the narrative as a way to universalize one's personal experiences with others.

A memoir is different than autoethnography because it starts with the writer's life rather than with the lives and activities of others; it is up to the writer to look inward, not outward. In SPN, the researcher chooses to self-interrogate rather than create interview questions for examining the inner and outer lives of others. Bradley and Nash suggest there is no set formula for self-interrogation in SPN writing because self is different; therefore, the personal narrative questions will be different. SPN begins with a "sample of one"—the SPN writer.[44] To make sense of the "raw material of life," Nash and Bradley suggest memoir and SPN differ in one essential way: memoirs are more informal and less scholarly, whereas SPN is less "free-floating and anecdotal" and more scholarly and focused.[45]

Nash and Bradley suggest that personal narrative essays come closest to SPN writing because authors use the mask that they present to the world in order to explore a topic and as a form of self-explanation. They describe essay writing as weighing or testing out some idea or hypothesis in a nontechnical way. The personal narrative essay tells the story of the author in such a way to analyze, interpret, and reflect upon some larger idea, event, or important figure in the writer's life.[46] One major ingredient that is missing in narrative essay writing is relating the personal narratives to themes that are universal to other groups like you have in SPN writing. In my SPN, the key themes were outsider/insider adapting in two worlds, moral courage, SHEROs, and transformation, which will be universalized in my narrative as an experience that other Black women can identify within their own experiences. The key to understanding my own personal and professional development as a leader has been a need to understand the role of women in executive leadership positions and the strategies they have used to navigate workplace dilemmas.[47] Nash and Bradley describe autobiographies as being more chronological and linear in structure and format, more historical and sweeping, than essays and memoirs.[48] Autobiographies tend to follow stricter, comprehensive timelines with a clear cut beginning, middle, and end, whereas SPN does not follow this rigid structure.

Overall one of the major differences between SPN and other approaches (autoethnography, memoirs, personal narrative, and autobiographies) is that SPN writing can take many different forms, while it retains its own scholarly uniqueness. SPN embraces all of the following qualities:

- While it is personal, it is also social.
- While it is practical, it is also theoretical.
- While it is reflective, it is also public.
- While it is local, it is also political.
- While it narrates, it also proposes.
- While it is self-revealing, it also evokes self-examination from readers.[49]

Nash and Bradley further suggest that an SPN's central purpose is to make an impact on both writer and reader, on both the individual and the community. Its overall goal, repeated in many different ways, is to find ways to incorporate the full body of human experiences into more traditional forms of research and scholarship.[50]

I selected SPN methodology because I believe society has much to learn from the stories of Black women like me. As suggested by John W. Creswell, narrative research design is a research strategy that is used to study the lives of one or more individuals to provide stories about their lives. The information is retold or re-storied by the researcher into a narrative chronology. The finished product is a combination of the views from the participant's life (or lives) and the researcher's life (or lives) that is combined in a collaborative narrative.[51] Nash and Bradley assert, "All SPN research begins and ends with a sample of one—the SPN writer."[52] Furthermore, Nash suggests personal narrative writing "helps us all to understand our histories, shapes our destinies ... [and] when done in an intellectual and emotionally respectable way, personal narrative writing can result in stunning self-insights."[53]

I applied the following steps in my pre-search phase.

Step one: To what extent are my experiences similar to my reader's experience? My experiences will shed light on an unrepresented population of women like me in the literature. While research has been done on women in higher education, I have found very little research on women whose experiences have been comparable to mine. I believe my journey, while it is unique, will appeal to a population of Black women like me who aspire to make similar transformations in their personal and professional lives. I believe my story will appeal to a broad population of women, and I hope that women like me will learn from my narrative as well as those who are aspiring to be leaders, such as women who have not benefited from formal and informal mentorships, women who aspire to start or complete their education, and men and women who supervise or mentor women like me. As suggested by Bradley, I will elucidate as much as possible the universal meanings and focus on the larger themes, principles, motifs, and learning of my experiences rather than simply recounting the actual sequence of events that make up my personal experiences that autobiographies contain.[54]

Step two: How can I create an engaging narrative encompassing my life and professional experiences in a way that overlaps with the professional narrative of my readers? Bradley asserts that the concept of narrative overlap applies to sameness, which is based on identicalness, likeness, homogeneity, and the uniformity of the narrative. Bradley suggests the former conveys the more universal human experience, whereas the latter suggests that we will not be able to find common ground unless we have the exact same experience. This statement helped to affirm for me just how important it is for my marginalized voice to be heard.

I will be explicit in my findings and provide personal examples, next steps, implications, areas for further study, and conclusions, all of which will be essential to the universalizability of my work. I want you to understand my life and experiences through my narrative as well as be able to have greater insight into your own narrative. I believe I will accomplish this if you come away with a sense of a shared experience through the examples I use in my personal and professional stories.

One example of doing this will be in the "we-search" of my writing when I share some of the experiences I have had dealing with stress brought on from working in hostile working environments and the coping strategies I used to navigate those challenges (even though I presented the face that I needed to at the time) and how I have supported others such as my family, friends, and employees. I will encourage others to think about this and relate it to their own experiences. I will encourage you to seek your own inner truth and authentic self. An example

Bradley used was universal for others because most of us have been sick in our lifetime.

Step three: How do I identify, and convey to you, the implications for your own field of study? I will ensure this happens when I convey the implications of my study as described earlier. It will be clear from my research what the implications are for my audience; I will include a section in my SPN (asserting my story in the research literature will contribute to the void of literature on Black women in leadership).

Step four: How do I universalize my findings to others in such a way that my "I" can co-exist with the "we" who are reading my work? I will always keep my audience central in my writing. Unlike memoir writing, where the author lets the chips fall where they may, I will make it a point to pick up the personal chips in order to show my relevance to others by spelling out the universalizability in my research.[55] As suggested by Bradley and Nash, I will tell my story through my writing with clarity, focus, and cogency. By exploring my research topic through the "I," then broadening my experiences and personal implications to capture the "we" in my narrative, I hope to build a shared closer relationship between you and me.[56]

I will also write letters in my manuscript. The use of letters in an SPN manuscript was introduced by Christian L. Berry in her thesis and is referred to as Epistle Scholarly Personal Narrative (ESPN).[57] An epistle is a "letter or message sent to an individual or group that is somewhat lengthy and instructive," and Nash and Bradley believe the insertion of letters authored by the writer in a manuscript should come as no surprise.[58] Berry suggested this style of writing as a way to recognize the "other" in your writing.[59]

There are three forms of epistolary writing: (1) monologic epistolary writings are told from one character's point of view; (2) dialogic epistolary writing tells the story through the back and forth correspondence of two characters; and (3) polylogic epistolary involves the telling of a story from multiple perspectives.[60] My letters will be told from a monologic perspective. Other forms of epistolary works are diary entries, journal writing, emails, blogs, and chatroom conversations. I will insert the following letters in my manuscript: to my mother, from my father to myself, to other Black women, and finally to PWIs to further ground my personal and professional narratives.

Letter to SPN

Dear SPN,

In this letter, I will utilize my narratives to provide a framework to you, the reader, that will provide greater insight into the recurring themes flowing throughout my work: outsider/insider adapting in two worlds, moral courage, SHEROs, and transformation, as well as HOME/family, faith in oneself, lack of mentors, cement ceiling/upward mobility, self-advocacy/social justice, and the responsibility of giving back.

My first experience with SPN was during an independent study course that I designed with Robert Nash. I selected this research methodology because I was very curious about this red-headed stepchild in the family of research methodology. My doctoral program required me to take qualitative/quantitative methodology courses as part of the core program. The SPN writing course was only offered in Fall session. I was on a fast track; I thought I could figure it out on my own by reading Robert's books on SPN. I opted to do the independent study without the SPN course.

Although my SPN was successfully completed, I know now that I put myself at a disadvantage by not taking the course first. If you are thinking about using SPN writing, I highly recommend taking the SPN writing course with Robert before embarking on the writing journey. It was not until I took the course that I began to finetune my SPN writing style.

SPN, like most nonrelated additions to a family, the research community has been slow to embrace you like your sister qualitative and your brother quantitative. Nonetheless, you have over the years developed a following with the student community and, more recently, the academic community at the University of Vermont. Your writing style and methodology is being presented throughout the academic community by its founder Robert Nash and his protégée DeMethra Bradley.

In this book, I will share how, in the beginning, I questioned whether I belonged in the doctoral program and if I had anything to contribute to the body of scholarly literature worthy of studying. Through your writing and methodology, my narratives have been grounded in the literature to produce research that will add to the growing body of research on Black women in higher education leadership. You have enabled me to conceptualize my personal and professional life and to review the oppression, challenges, struggles, and, yes, successes that I have encountered during my journey from housekeeper to director to Doctor of Education.

This writing has been therapeutic and insightful for me as I continue on my professional journey. My newfound writing skills will enable me as a practitioner to write about my experiences in the academy and add to the growing body of research on leadership, mentoring, cultural competency, and Black women in higher education. I believe SPN methodology is a valuable resource for women like me to use to conduct continued research regarding their experiences in the academy as students, leaders, and faculty. You have taught me there is value in everyone's story. Everyone deserves to be heard.

Finally, I offer the following tips for anyone who aspires to be an SPN writer.

- Have faith that your story has value.
- Find a writing partner.
- Find a dedicated physical space to write.
- Schedule time to meet with your writing partner.
- Write, then edit.
- End each writing session with a start point for your next writing session.
- Let your scholarship compliment your writing, not the other way around.
- Be creative and open to what you learn about yourself along the way.
- Know that SPN is therapeutic.
- Have FUN!

I hope these tips will serve as a resource for aspiring SPN writers.

Best wishes,

Leslye

Chapter Three: Kornegay Journey to Housekeeper

You can never leave HOME. You take it with you no matter where you go. HOME is between your teeth, under your fingernails, in the hair follicles, in your smile, in the ride of your hips, in the passage of your breast. HOME is in every sentence of your writing.

—Maya Angelou[61]

HOME Narrative

The first four years of my life were spent relocating often to various places across the United States and even overseas to Tokyo, Japan. When I reflect back on those times in my life, they are always filled with a sense of joy and happiness.

When I was four, my family returned to the states to make our new HOME on the Langley Air Force Base in Virginia's Chesapeake Bay. Our high-rise apartment building was right on the waterfront by the Officers' Club. I was drawn to the water and white sands. My favorite times were playing with my younger brother along the water's edge, dodging jellyfish and crabs and catching turtles for pets. My father even bought me a goldfish and let me keep her in my bedroom. I named her Goldie.

I was not your typical little girl. I am told I was cute; I had long braids and eyes that changed from hazel to brown, depending on my mood. I was often referred to as my father's child. Anything that was girly was not for me. One might say I was a tomboy, but then so was my mom. Society was not very kind to tomboys back then. It still isn't.

I guess my mother was trying to protect me because she knew society would frown on a little girl who did not act like a little girl was supposed to act. Before my parents divorced, my father spent a lot of his time with me. He was my hero, so it was only natural that I would want to be like him. I would not play with dolls; that is probably why, to this day, I cannot style my own hair and do not like to go shopping. Nor did I like the pretend kitchen with the stove and refrigerator, which is probably why I am still not very good when it comes to putting a meal together. Whenever I was forced to wear a dress in public, I would secretly wear shorts under it.

Even at a young age, I was strong-willed, independent, and desired to live outside of the norms of traditional girlhood. Sometimes, when my mom got on my nerves, I would roll my eyes at her, but I only did it when my dad was around because I knew he would protect me. My mom would banish me to my bedroom, but first she would threaten to spank me if my dad did not do it first. And so, he would follow me to my room, close the door behind him, and laugh. "Leslye, what am I going to do with you? Why do you give your mother such a hard time?" He never laid a hand on me. Yes, he had spoiled me rotten. Remembering these moments with him brings me to tears now.

Not too long after we moved to Virginia, my mother divorced my father, and he eventually divorced my siblings and me as well. As the first born, I was old enough to have memories with him that my siblings do not share, so it was especially difficult for me. After the divorce, I only saw my father during summer vacation, and things changed even more when he started another family. We never had the same kind of close relationship again. This was the first of many significant transformations that I would experience in my personal life.

As a child, I was angry with my mother for a long time. In my mind, it was her fault because she was the one who had taken me and my siblings and moved. Although I loved my mother dearly, we had a tumultuous relationship until I was old enough to understand that she was more than just a wife to my father and a mother to my siblings and me. Even though she wanted us to be happy, she was not going to stay in an unhappy marriage just for the sake of her children.

An unhappy Black woman divorcing a good provider was practically unheard of in the 1960s, but there must have been something in the water back in the early 1960s because four of my maternal grandmother's eight children divorced their spouses and moved back HOME, kids and all. At one point, 14 grade-school-aged children lived in that three-bedroom house. To this day, I still don't really know where we all slept. Living in those close quarters, my first cousins became like my sisters and brothers; we formed lifelong bonds during those years.

My maternal grandmother—we called her Ninny—was the backbone of our family, like so many Black women before her. She and her husband were the only grandparents I have ever known. Although my grandfather lived in the HOME and worked odd jobs, what I recall about him more than anything was that he did hard labor for the railroad and, on his time off, he liked to enjoy the spirits. We have generational abuse of the spirits among the men in my extended family, and my grandfather conformed to that pattern. So, he left the running of the household and the rearing of the children to Ninny. This is a familiar scene in Black communities. It's common for Black women to be the thread that binds the family together.[62]

Even though my mom was a vital influence in raising my siblings and me, she relied on my grandmother to help, and Ninny left lasting impressions, greatly influencing my childhood development. She was an independent, courageous Black woman in the post-1960 South, modeling a strong work ethic, values, and commitment to family, courage, independence, and resilience. My mother got her zest for life from Ninny, and she in turn passed it on to me.

Terri Hurdle, a Black doctoral student and professional at the University of Cincinnati, wrote about the influence her own grandmother had on her during her childhood.

> As a young child under the auspices of my grandmother (Mama), I can recall her utilizing different tactics to motivate me. They would range from a monetary reward, words of affirmation, or an inspirational speech. Her most prevalent tactic was the encouragement quote and/or what I understood to be scripture later in life like verses Philippians 4:19, "I can do all things through Christ which strengthens me." Statements such as "Work

hard and you will be successful," "The early bird catches the worm," and "If you ask, seek, and knock, the door will be opened" were stated quite often.[63]

I do not remember a time when my grandmother was not working outside of the HOME. Ninny had a full-time job working for the state mental institution. Back then, a state job offered more security than it might these days. That's how she was able to be the family's breadwinner. Furthermore, her father had left some land to all of his children when he passed, and Ninny used her portion of land to farm and raise livestock that provided most of the food for the table, all looked after by her eight children. Ninny's father was a White Irishman, and his mother was an orphan with Native American features. My grandmother always reminded us that her people had never been slaves in this country. Regardless, her birth certificate described her as Black. It seems, the word Negro was not used on birth certificates until the 1930s.[64] My grandfather was also of mixed race. His mother—we called her Grandma Pinky— had been pure Blackfoot Indian.

I recall when I was old enough to notice that some members of my family did not look like me. So, I asked my mom why some of them appeared White and had red hair and green eyes, while others were brown like mine with light brown eyes. Why did we all look so different? My mother explained that my ancestors were Irish, Native American, and Black, and that the Black heritage we shared is what determined our race as Black. I can recall even as a child finding something very wrong with that answer, but it had to be correct if my mother said so.

When I was old enough to learn that my birth certificate labeled me as a Negro female born to Negro parents, I questioned it again. During the 1960s, the color of the parents' skin prompted the labeling of the child's race at birth; my birth certificate is a prime example. This stemmed from the days of chattel slavery. If you had "one drop" of Black blood, you were considered a Negro.

My experience has been that this is still true today in some regard, but the categories have broadened in scope, and Negro is sometimes referred to as African American, Black, or most recently person of color. I am not sure when this happened in our history, but I have often wondered why the term "person of color" is socially acceptable, whereas in my community there was a period in our history when calling someone "colored" was not socially acceptable.

I suppose this goes back to slavery days when lighter-skinned Blacks were forced to work in the master's house and were considered by the Black community to have a level of status above the slaves who worked in the fields.[65] This belief continues to be communicated in the media and society at large. Lighter-skinned women are believed to glean more marriage proposals and more success in the workplace than darker-skinned women.[66] I recall hearing stories from elder family members about the Brown Paper Bag Test—the Jim Crow era practice of comparing one's skin color to a brown bag to determine one's level of acceptance in both the Black and White communities.

Additionally, passing for White in the North was another testing ground for some people of color. I have a number of people on my mother's side of the family who look White and/or Native American, including my mother—though she never tried to pass for White. Prior to the civil rights movement, it was common for some of my ancestors to live double lives, passing as White up North. When I got older, I met a couple of them; they looked like my mom. They always recognized the "otherness" among themselves, but they considered themselves to be first and foremost Black.

When I was seven, my mother moved our family to an apartment community called Green Acres in Goldsboro, North Carolina. Funnily enough, a TV show back then called *Green Acres* starred Eva Gabor as one of the leading actresses, portraying a very high society White woman with polished city ways. Her husband buys a farm with animals and everything else included, so the city girl must learn to survive in the country, in spite of it all.

Like Eva, my mom plopped me and my siblings on the very edge of town with the closest community being an Air Force base. What I remember most about the people in our neighborhood was that everyone was struggling. It was a segregated housing community, post-1968. The buildings were one level, almost military barrack style.

Our neighborhood had a lot of trees, which I used to love to climb. One day, I climbed a tree so high no one would come up after me. My mom ended up calling the fire department, which came with their trucks and ladder to bring me back to safety. Looking back, I am not sure where I was trying to go, but I felt at peace away from everything. It was just the tree, Mother Nature, and me. That particular time, I was dressed in my Easter Sunday best—a dress my mother's new boyfriend had bought for me, with my white windowpane stockings and white patent leather shoes. I ruined the entire outfit.

At that time, my mother was working for General Electric. Although it was difficult for her as a single parent, she wanted to provide a HOME for her children. I know now that my mother struggled to put food on the table and to keep a roof over our heads. As an adult, I learned that my father sent my mother only $75 a month in alimony and child support for all three of us until we turned 18 years old. Still, my mother never said anything negative about our father to us.

We were poor, but my mother always made sure we never went to bed hungry, had a roof over our heads, wore clean clothes free of holes, and were well-groomed. She did not believe in accepting assistance from social service agencies, and she was able to keep our family together without welfare until she remarried when I was nine years old. She modeled for me at a young age what it means to be a strong Black woman.

Mr. Mack, my new step-father, had been okay for my mother's boyfriend, but I was not happy that she married him. I was very vocal about it. I was angry because I felt that he was trying to replace my father. Imagine a nine year-old telling adults something like that. We laugh about it now, but it was not funny to me back then. I took my role seriously as the eldest of my mother's children. I believed it was my responsibility to look out for my mom and my siblings because my dad was not with us.

My mom depended on me a lot to help around the house, being a single parent who had to work to provide for her family. Her early confidence in my abilities helped me accept responsibility at such a young age. I was a "latchkey kid." Unlike the stereotype that has been attached to this phrase, I believe I was a very responsible, mature nine year-old. If and when I got into mischief, I generally ended up only hurting myself. I was never a danger to anyone else.

Looking back, I guess I acted out to get attention. I knew if I showed my butt enough times, my mom would show me the same kind of love her parents showed her—a good old-fashioned whipping. I recall those experiences like it was yesterday. She would tell me to go and pick my own punishment, which meant go pick a switch for her to whip me. When I think about those days, the past comes rushing back to me with a flood of memories. I would always try to find a switch from a tree branch that looked old and withered because the green ones hurt like hell, and I would take my time peeling it. My mom knew how to give a whipping without leaving permanent marks.

Years later, I would joke with my mother about those whippings and share with her that it is called child abuse these days. Who would have thought she could have gone to jail for not sparing the rod? Is it not mentioned in the Bible somewhere, "Spare the rod, spoil the child"?

As an adult, I understood that corporal punishment was the only way my mom knew how to prepare me for a world that would not tolerate a sassy Black girl. She was trying to teach me to stay in my place like her mother had taught her to do. In *The Color Purple,* Celie tells her stepson, Harpo, that he needs to show his wife, Sophia, who wears the pants in their family by beating her because she needs to know her place as his wife. Her rationale for giving him that kind of advice is simply that it is all she has ever known with any man, including her husband. Celie equates love with a beating.

I speak of Celie here to illustrate why I believe my mom used tough love to discipline me; I was after all her first born so naturally she was harder on me.

Additionally, in some ways, the challenges, obstacles, and barriers presented to me by the caring elders in my life like my mother could be attributed to the kinds of issues they wanted me to be able to navigate when I got older. I was born during a period in our history that allowed me to experience both segregation and integration and also both the civil rights movement and the women's rights movement in my lifetime. My mom's intentions were good, and she taught me how to be a strong Black woman, granted via traditional methods. It is probably a good thing that I learned not to be passive because I would need to continue to challenge the status quo as an adult.

To ensure my step-father did not replace my father, I refused to call him dad or father. I had been told to call him Mr. Mack before he and my mother married, and I continued to call him Mr. Mack after they were married. Mr. Mack never deserved my anger; he was a good man and a good provider. I know he must have really loved my mother to put up with me and my siblings. It would take years for me to remove my blinders imposed by my child-self to realize who had really been there for me all along. He is really the man who helped my mother raise her children. I know now while they were not perfect, they did the best that they could. Interestingly, my father remarried during this time to a woman who already had children, then they had one together.

When I reflect back upon that time in my childhood, I remember how much change happened when I turned nine years old. My step-father was also in the military, and that year he received orders to be stationed in Tokyo, Japan. Of course, he took his new family with him. That would be my second time living in Tokyo, but it would be different than the first because I was old enough to remember the experience of living in another culture.

Being raised in the military had a significant impact on my developmental years from the age of 9 through 13. Our new life in Japan was dramatically different from my mother's HOMEtown where she had moved us when she left my father.

We lived on Grand Heights Air Force Base in Tokyo, which was one of many military bases scattered throughout Japan at the time.

In 1969, Tokyo was one of the largest cities in the world. Even though it was more than 50 years ago, I can remember it like it was yesterday. The city was filled with an indescribable energy. If I had to choose a time in my life where I could go back, it would be Tokyo in 1969. I loved everything Japanese, from the language, to the foods, the customs, the clothes, and above all, the people.

I quickly adjusted to the culture and bonded with an older Japanese lady named Sodoko. She was the girlfriend of one of my parents' friends, and she became like a big sister to me. She really exposed me to Japanese culture outside of the military base, teaching me about Japanese customs. I often spent the night with her and her family in their HOME. I embraced that totally different world like it was my own. I attribute my positive childhood experience overseas to my ability to embrace other cultures and ethnic groups. These childhood experiences provided a foundation for me to value international and domestic diversity as an adult.

Every time my family relocated to a different military base, which was every two to four years, I learned to adapt to the change. Always the new kid on the block, it did not take me too long to learn who the various personalities were at every new location. The same characters would show up— similar personalities, but different people. I learned never to become too attached to anything or anyone because I knew I would not be there permanently and would have to leave one day. In a number of ways, my childhood was vastly different from someone who had lived in the same location all of their childhood and had the same friends from kindergarten to high school.

Sometimes I had to attend two different schools in one academic year. That might explain why my mom did not find out I was deaf in one ear until I was in second grade, which was probably caused by an ear infection I had as a toddler. When I had to have my ear infections treated, I used to sit on my dad's lap so the doctor could insert a syringe into my ear without any sedation. My dad was the only person who could handle me. That was one of the ways I learned to tolerate pain at a very young age, and it's also why I have a fear of needles to this day.

Suffice it to say, some critical learning did not happen during the years prior to my hearing loss being detected, which greatly impacted my confidence with certain subjects in school. I believe my love for stories and reading took off during this time. Books helped me escape reality, where I was separated from my father, and they transported me to the place I would be rescued by my prince. Of course, my prince was really my father—the man I hoped would one day arrive on his white horse, battle anyone who meant me harm, save the day, and take me away to live with him forever and ever.

In elementary school, my favorite pastime was storytelling in the school library. Later I would graduate to reading about superheroes like Wonder Woman and Cat Woman, then magicians like Merlin. I was a dreamer, forever musing about something—and distinguishing myself more and more as an outsider. Only occasionally would I surface back to earth from my occasional fantasy trips and read something with substance.

When I was in the fourth grade, I read at a twelfth grade level. I commonly read multiple books at the same time. As a child, I loved history, but I recall experiencing a cultural disconnect from learning after the fifth grade.[67] As I got older, it seemed as though except for a few Black people who made it into the history books, there were no new faces or stories told. It was not until years later, as a young adult, when I took control of my learning, that I became exposed to the rich history of Black people that was not in mainstream history books. This is one area that I believe a segregated experience during my formative years would have benefited my education as a young Black person.

Later in life, I learned that my parents had assumed I got a better education in integrated schools than they received in a segregated school. However, the schools on military bases in the 1960s and 1970s were more in line with lower middle-class schools.[68] They were also all integrated. My parents did not understand that the "better" education I received meant learning about the Black American experience through the White American lens.

I mastered basic math and English and found it very easy to memorize formulas, numerical series, and phone numbers. But, I struggled with some advanced coursework. My struggles with English were punctuations and grammatical errors. In math, geometry and statistics both came easily to me while I struggled with algebra. Although I persevered, that was when I started to develop phobias about algebra and grammar. I convinced myself I could not do these things and literally ran from them during that stage in my life.

During this phase of my life, I learned to read lips and developed the art of active listening. In time, my one good ear began to compensate for my deaf ear. This felt like nothing short of a miracle. Even now, unless I disclose my disability, people are surprised to learn that I have hearing loss and eyesight challenges. I was severely bullied in middle school and college. This did not help my outside experience.

Our military family's constant moving, my hearing loss and eyesight diagnosis in fourth grade, and my parent's divorce forced me to learn how to adapt to change at a very young age. That would become a valuable asset later in life, but it had its downside as well. At times, I felt like an outsider, not truly having a HOME base because I always knew the changes were not permanent. In Windy Paz-Armor's SPN, she describes my image of HOME, reminding me of those times when my child-self endured the constant relocations my family made when I was growing up.

> HOME or the image of HOME for me has served as
> a remembering tool.
> HOME is my mother cooking something from the
> freshest of ingredients
> that tastes even better than what it smells.
> HOME is a community of women working, loving,
> and healing together.[69]

As I unpack my image of HOME, I am reminded of all the cherished memories I hold dear, regardless of where we lived. I can no longer return to the HOME I knew during my childhood—except in my memory and in my dreams. HOME for me starts from the inside. Experiences are ingrained in my memory, like the jazz music records and cassettes my step-father used to play. Every time I hear those familiar tunes, I think about HOME. I brought HOME with me to Vermont.

HOME is where I learned how to value people based on their personalities and not their race, ethnicity, sexual orientation, gender, religion, or ethnic group. Those images of HOME remind me of how I learned to play team sports alongside doing gymnastics and running track. The skills I developed playing team sports helped me to build interpersonal relationships and taught me how to win or lose gracefully. They have served me well into adulthood.

The first Black teacher I ever had was in Japan when I was 10. Her name was Mrs. Kennedy. She was a no-nonsense instructor who taught introductory typing. She focused a lot of time and attention on me, determined to have me master the skill. Under Mrs. Kennedy, I learned how to type with black tape on the typewriter letters to help me memorize the keyboard. After learning from her, I never needed another typing course, and to this day, I can still type without looking at the keys. Mrs. Kennedy made such a huge impact on me that she is the only teacher I can remember by name. The typing skills she taught me became valuable assets later in life.

When I was 11, I began my spiritual walk. Back then, there was no Black church on Grant Heights Military Base. My father was Baptist, my mom was Catholic, and my step-father was Methodist. My stepmother was Holiness. Even though I was baptized Catholic when I was born, my parents had promised themselves they would not force their children into church, but they also would not discourage us from attending. Eventually, I was curious enough to seek out church, but my experience was cold and unwelcoming. That one experience made a lasting impression on me.

The base community was predominately White. There were a few Black families and many households were interracial, but I am not sure where these folks worshiped. All I know is the day I went to church, none of them were there. I remember the congregation being unwelcoming and cold. The church was full of White people singing these god-awful hymns that had no rhythm. The sermon was delivered without the vigor often found in Black churches. I did not stay through the service, and it was the last time I would attend church in Japan or anywhere else. I would have more experiences on my spiritual walk as I got older.

When I reflect back upon our time in Japan, I am reminded that the protected world we lived in on base was not indicative of the world we left behind in the United States. The closest tie we had to US Black culture was each other and *Soul Train*, which came on television once a week. Everything else was in Japanese.

In August 1974, we returned to the United States. I was 13 years old and entering the seventh grade. We were all so excited about returning stateside, seeing our family again, and getting back to enjoying life as we had known it before going to Japan. I did not see much on that trip because I had broken my eyeglasses playing tetherball right before we left. What I do recall is a huge, two-level Boeing 747—the biggest plane I had ever been on. It even had a movie theater on board. I recall thinking, *Surely this plane is too heavy to fly us all the way to Hawaii and then to California.*

The Air Force (and so my parents) moved us from one of the largest cities in the world to one of the smallest towns in North Carolina. The town had one DANG stoplight and one general store. It did not take me long to realize the life we had just left in Japan would be some of the most cherished memories of my childhood.

My teenage years were filled with growing pains. Returning to the States was a culture shock for me. I was a teenager who had been used to a very full, active life in Japan. My parents had given me the freedom to explore the culture and the country and do things that would impact my ability to adapt later in life. At 10, I was traveling all over Japan with my friends—a lot of it was unchaperoned, independent exploration. There was a lot of trust on all levels because we were not living in the real world. It was a fabricated American world on an Air Force base in a foreign country. I could go to live concerts, night movies, weekend school field trips, and sleepovers with friends on and off base.

When we returned to North Carolina, I think my parents suddenly realized that, though I was only 13, I had grown into a young woman along the way. I no longer had the freedom to come and go like I had in Japan. I was shy and quiet during this time. I applied the same coping strategies in my new location that I had in the past. It did not take me long to figure out the different personalities. To complicate matters, my best friend at the time taught me how to smoke cigarettes. My picking up the nasty habit at 13 probably had a lot to do with the amount of free time I had without parental supervision while my parents were working, the very description of a "latchkey kid." I am not sure why my parents were surprised. They both smoked cigarettes, and we had moved to the tobacco capital of America.

Moreover, my summer job was harvesting in tobacco barns. It was hard work for a teenager, but it paid good money. I was making $100 a day barning tobacco. That was not bad for six hours of work back in 1975. Back then, many adults did not earn that kind of money. I worked for relatives some of the time and other times for White farmers who my grandmother knew would not mistreat Black workers.

I developed a strong work ethic while working in the fields along with my cousins during the summer. I made enough money to buy my own school clothes every year. My parents did not dictate to me how much money I was allowed to spend on clothes or what I could wear to school. Thankfully, I had good taste even then.

During the school year, I would bag groceries at the military base commissary, basically working for tips. My mom had always told me to give a 100 percent effort regardless of the work, so that is what I did. My customers noticed. I got to know them well, and they would request me specifically when they came to the commissary.

I am thankful that my parents allowed me to work and earn my own money at such a young age. It helped me to understand the importance of money. According to my mom, it was important for me to learn how to take care of myself, not to depend on anyone to do it for me. I recall her saying, "Once you can take care of yourself, then get married." So, as a teen, though I did not *need* to work, I *wanted* to work.

My mother and step-father did quite well financially, which is why it was not necessary for me to have a job. Mr. Mack had retired from the military and started working a blue-collar job at a local electric company, and my mother was a social worker at the state mental institution. We moved to a middle-class Black neighborhood where teachers and doctors lived. There, I made some lifelong friends, became an Alpha Kappa Alpha (AKA) debutant, and was introduced to society (Black Society) when I was 16.

Team sports became my focus again during my teenage years. I joined the girls' basketball team in the eighth grade, and that is when I truly began to blossom. Middle school had been a rough transition for me because I was often bullied and kept to myself a lot. Eventually, the bullies found someone else to pick on, my shyness wore off, and I learned to stand up for myself. Playing team sports also helped me open up to other people and taught me how to operate as a member of a team as opposed to relying only on my own wit. It helped me to develop more interpersonal relationships and to understand the value that every individual brings to any given situation.

With a team, I did not have to be the one to score every basket; if my team member scored, I scored. I learned that winning is not everything; sometimes you can lose and still be a winner. It's about *how* you play the game. My strong commitment, valuing my team members, and my dedication to the sport won me a lot of recognition amongst my peers.

Although I knew a lot of people, I only had a few close friends. This would continue into high school. I would become more active and popular (pom-pom girl, varsity cheerleader, and basketball), but I was still an introvert. Later in life, I would learn to perform extroversion when I needed to.

I was an introvert at HOME as well. When I spoke, it was because I had something to say, and people generally listened. When others spoke, they captured my full attention because I often read lips due to my hearing loss. This helped me develop exceptional listening skills as well as enabled me to give audiences my full attention with continuous eye contact.

College was not something I even thought about until my senior year of high school. Much of my family's focus was on my older step-brother, who was an all-American in football, basketball, and track. It was assumed that he would go to college on an athletic scholarship.

I never felt like I was the brightest child in our family. I always thought my younger brother or sister would be the doctors in our family. They both scored exceptionally high on their IQ tests (borderline geniuses), plus my brother was able to recite any athletic statistic and knew the King James Bible and the Koran frontward and backward. Although they are both exceptionally intelligent and attended some college, neither finished and have done well for themselves.

When I put my mind to anything, I can excel. I just have to commit. In high school, I had to take geometry twice, not because I could not understand geometry the first time around, but because the teacher did not care whether or not I learned geometry. So, I zoned out. I was heavily into romantic magazines back then, like *Truth or Consequences*. One day, I had a magazine tucked inside my geometry book and I was so engrossed in my reading that the teacher caught me. My hearing failed me that day. Her name was Mrs. Kennedy as well. (I only remember her name because it was the same as my typing teacher.) Unlike the Mrs. Kennedy who taught me how to type, the Mrs. Kennedy who taught geometry blamed me for not being fully engaged in her classroom, as opposed to blaming her lackluster teaching style. After that day, I could do nothing right, and I did not pass the class. That was the first time I had ever flunked anything in my life.

My second geometry teacher taught me the fundamentals of geometry that have stayed with me to this day. I earned a B+ in her class. What a difference teaching style makes. I committed to passing geometry, and I did so with flying colors!

One of the findings from the article, "The Achievement Gap: Myth and Reality" suggested the highest level of mathematics a student has studied will have the strongest effect on their degree completion.[70] In regards to my own experience, this proved to be false.

Senior year, I decided to enroll in honors English and literature classes. It was the first time these courses were taught by a young husband and wife team in my school. It was also the first time I had taken a course in North Carolina where I was the only Black student in the class. I was a little concerned at first, but the teachers really made me feel at HOME. Their teaching style was very contemporary, introducing modern themes into their curriculum to help present the material to the class. This teaching style allowed me to excel.

I recall one time, early in the semester, they played a song and asked the class what the name of it was. I was the only person to answer correctly. It was "We are the Champions," and I knew this because my step-brother used to listen to Queen all the time. I think I gained some capital with my teacher and my White classmates that day. We found we had some common ground; it helped to break the ice. We would go on to build some strong relationships. Those two courses changed the course of my life because I literally had not thought about life after high school until then.

Preparing for college was one of those times in my life where a mentor would have been beneficial. Years later, my mom shared with me that she did not have a clue about how to help prepare me for college. She really felt that the school guidance counselors were better equipped to guide me in preparing for college and the application process. We both know now that did not happen. I never went to visit any schools with my parents before I applied. I just applied and was accepted into an all Black college. I had no idea what to expect. It would be an experience of a lifetime. I had never been around so many Black people at one time in my life.

Even though I thrived academically and socially, it was not a good environment for me; I enjoyed the social life a little too much. I knew I would fail if I did not make a change in my life. My young adult-self did a really hard thing back then; after two years, I decided to leave college. I was financially dependent upon my parents, and I was not able to get financial aid because my step-father made too much money at his white-collar job, so my parents paid cash for me to go to college. By the time I decided to leave, my parents were also paying for my younger brother's college education. In part, I dropped out because I felt like I was taking money away from the family. Looking back now, I know that I made the right decision. This was a pivotal point in my life.

The first real social-security paying job I ever had was selling shoes at a very popular clothing store. I was good at it, but I had a desire to really spread my wings. So, I eventually moved to New Jersey with my mom's older sister and her family. In the early 1980s, the economy was devastated with the Savings and Loan Crisis, which created an economic recession. It was hard to get a job without a college degree.[71] That should have been enough to make me think about going back to school, but I was determined I would be an exception.

It took months of pounding the pavement, but I finally landed a union housekeeping job at the Playboy Hotel and Casino in Atlantic City, New Jersey. I was disappointed that was the only work that I could find. I had never aspired to be a housekeeper, and I did not know of anyone else who did either. The stigma around that type of work was prevalent.

It felt degrading to me because I thought it meant that I was not worthy of doing anything more with my life. That was the kind of work slaves were forced to do when they came to America. It was not the kind of work I felt I could be proud of, and it would take years for me to break out of that mindset. In the meantime, I decided that if I had to be a housekeeper, I would be the best damn housekeeper they ever had.

Housekeeping was easy work compared to some of the jobs I had performed as a child. The union contract only required me to clean thirteen rooms in eight hours. I earned a wage and very lucrative tips. I was permitted to take the whole eight hours to clean thirteen rooms, or I could take on more work and receive double the pay. Often, I completed the thirteen rooms within only three hours because I worked very fast and efficiently.

It did not take management long to offer me a supervisor job. I turned them down because I witnessed a lot of favoritism and practices in the management of the department that I did not want to be associated with. Two years later, I was laid off. But I'd had enough of my adventure away from my family anyway. So, I moved back to North Carolina in 1982.

I decided to finally go back to college and enrolled at a local university. This time I financed my education. I continued to work in hospitality as a front desk clerk for two major hotels. I experienced my first significant "-ism" when I applied for a front desk manager position. The top two candidates came down to my White college roommate, Arlene, and me. Management did not know we were roommates. We were both qualified for the job, but I had been there longer. I was also the only Black person working the front desk at that very prestigious hotel. Needless to say, my roommate got the job. I was called into the office of the front desk director, a White man, who told me that if I wanted to move up, then maybe I should look into housekeeping. He told me that he knew the housekeeping director on a first-name basis, and he was sure she could use me. He would put in a good word for me, he said. Soon, the director of housekeeping came looking for me.

That was one of those times when having a mentor who shared my racial identity to advise me would have been beneficial, especially because during that period in my life, I was not on the best terms with my mother.

My roommate was surprised they had given her the position. She offered to step down, but I told her not to. This was two years before the Civil Rights Act of 1991 was passed. The act detailed who had the burden of proof in certain cases and prescribed remedies in cases of discrimination based on race, color, religion, gender, age, disability, and national origin. It granted plaintiffs the right to a jury trial.[72] I felt helpless. I did not have the money to get a lawyer, and I did not know about the federal laws around Affirmative Action and Equal Opportunity (AAEO) at the time. So, I just accepted my fate and found myself working in housekeeping once again. I decided if I was going to be a housekeeping supervisor, I would be the best damn housekeeping supervisor I could be.

I spent five years in hotel management becoming one of the first Black executive housekeepers in the area. As an executive housekeeper, I worked in full-service hotels with 500 rooms and more than 100 employees in my department. During that time, I was studying sociology and psychology at North Carolina State University. My college coursework along with my prior role as a front-line housekeeper gave me instant credibility amongst my workforce. I had no mentors or role models who looked like me, so I often emulated the dominant leadership styles of my White male supervisors, who were traditional and authoritative.

At the height of my executive housekeeper trajectory in hotels, I was hired to open a 500-room full-scale property (similar to today's four-star hotel). The general manager who hired me was one of the best leaders I have ever worked for in the business. He was also the first non-White supervisor I'd ever had; he had a White father and a Mexican mother. I think he was ahead of his time as a down-to-earth, effective communicator who did not micromanage his employees. He knew that he had hired an expert when he hired me, and he gave me the freedom to do my job. He also cared about me on a personal level and encouraged me to develop my skills and knowledge through professional development. He could see my potential even before I could, and he wanted me to succeed beyond the role he had hired me for. His evaluation process helped me to become a better leader, rather than simply emulating the White men I had worked for. He would tell me, "You are only as good as your weakest link. Help your weakest link become stronger, and the team will perform better." I use this philosophy to this day.

The role modeling that supervisor demonstrated was exceptional. I recall when one of my employee's house burned down, and that general manager went out of his way to come up with funds so we could help them set up a new household. During that time, I began to develop my own philosophy about management and treating employees the way that they wanted to be treated, as opposed to the way that I wanted to treat them. Employees worked for the hotel at will, which meant they could not be let go without a cause. I have had to terminate a lot of employees, but I never had one challenge my termination because I always let employees know where they stood with their performance. It was never a surprise to them if they were let go.

Also during that time, I first dealt with the impact of the crack cocaine epidemic in the workplace. Drug paraphernalia was around the facility's public spaces, both inside and outside. I suspected one of the employees, but that was before drug testing became a condition of employment. Eventually, I was forced to terminate the employee due to poor performance. That was one of the first times I terminated someone and feared for my safety after. One day not long after letting Jeronald go, I was taking a call in my small office. He had come back to talk to me. His body blocked my office door. I felt trapped, but I did not panic. I stood, faced him straight on, and calmly asked, "Do you need something?"

He looked at me and said, "Miss Leslye. I just wanna say, I am sorry. I want to thank you for all that you have done for me. One day, when I get myself together, will you give me another chance?"

A wave of relief washed over me. I knew that I had done my best with him. My genuine caring about his welfare had reached him somehow. He had come back to thank me, not to hurt me.

I have rehired quite a few people after terminating them, and most of them were ready to commit to what they needed to do to keep their jobs the second time around. But rehiring did not work for everyone. I even had to fire my own brother. Against my better judgment, I hired my brother when he needed a job. It was not against company policy to hire family, but I had made it my own rule not to do so because sometimes family can be your worst employees. I had seen it happen to other people. One day, my brother challenged my authority in front of his peers and gave me no choice but to fire him. It left a lasting impression on my staff. They knew if I would fire my own brother, I would not hesitate to let them go as well.

My last hotel experience was not a pleasant one. After the general manager who hired me left the company, my days were numbered with his replacement who came in like a tyrant. He seemed determined that I was not going to work for him. I knew how to do my job, and I knew the concerns this manager had about me had nothing to do with my work, but with the fact that I was the only Black person on his leadership team. One day, he called me into his office and propositioned me for sex. I turned around and walked out.

It never occurred to me that I had to go through a formal process on the job to complain about the incident. My unemployment claim was denied as were my sexual harassment claims to the Federal Court of Appeals. I did all of the filing myself because I was naive back then, and it never occurred to me to get a lawyer. I could not afford one anyway. Once again, I felt helpless and alone. Having a mentor to guide me through this process would have been a blessing. I just did not have that kind of support. Six months after I walked out, several White women made sexual harassment complaints against him, and he finally was terminated.

That was probably the lowest point I had ever experienced as an adult and another pivotal point in my life. I went from being lower middle class and self-supporting, to no job and no income. Audre Lorde suggested in her book *Sister Outsider:*

> One of the most basic Black survival skills is the ability to change, to metabolize experience, good or ill, into something that is useful, lasting, effective. Four hundred years of survival as an endangered species has taught most of us that if we intend to live, we had better become fast learners.[73]

In order to survive, I became a fast learner.

That was one of the darkest times in my adult life. I literally had to pick myself up and start all over again from nothing. It would take me nine months to secure another job. Like Audre Lorde, I recall asking myself during this time in my life, "Why me?" What other creature in the world besides the Black woman has had to build the knowledge of so much hatred into her survival and keep going?"[74] I know of no other creature.

I resumed my spiritual walk during this time and found myself in church on New Year's Eve 1990. I did not have to hit a low point to go to church. I prayed every day, but I had not found a church HOME.

Before the year was out, I was working again. I began working for the State of North Carolina University system in 1990 as an entry level housekeeping supervisor on third shift. That was an eye-opening experience for me. Some interesting characters worked with me during that time. If you can endure the hours, life on third shift is like no other. As entry-level supervisor jobs go, I think that one was by far the best time for me. I worked with a team of housekeepers who were seasoned professionals. They knew their jobs, and they did them well. They also all worked other jobs to supplement their incomes.

The stereotype for third-shift workers was that they slept most of the shift and only worked the last two hours. I did not find this to be true. They were hard-working, dedicated professionals. They worked for the benefits and to send their children to school. While some of the staff was my age, I did not have one that aspired to be more than what they were at the time. They were perfectly content as they were. Unfortunately, there were no women in senior leadership. The department's senior management was a group of Black men and one White man. I applied several times and was passed over by less qualified men. I quickly realized if I wanted to grow, it would not happen there.

My second state job was with the public school system in Bedford County, the second largest school system in North Carolina. I was one of the first Black women to work as college campus weekend coordinator, and I soon became the only woman on the entire team. All of my peers were Black men, and my immediate supervisor was a Black man. There were no Black people beyond my supervisor's level in senior leadership. That would not change during the three years I was employed there.

As the only woman on the team, I was treated like one of the guys. I think what helped me survive was the fact that I did just as much work, if not more, than they did. They had to respect me. If they talked down to me, they only got away with it once. I carried myself the way that I expected them to treat me.

I was responsible for 20 schools, working with the principals and the head supervisors in those schools. Very early on, I learned that each school's personality and culture were reflected in its leadership. I applied the adapting skills that I had learned as a child, going into those schools as a member of the team. I was there to support the housekeepers and to help them be successful. If a principal had a problem with a housekeeping employee, I did not assume the principal was always right. I went in, observed, and based my conclusions on my own observations. If my observations differed from the principals, I had to have my facts together. I quickly developed a reputation with the principals for being competent and skilled in my support for their staff. The housekeepers viewed me as an advocate.

Many of the school system housekeeping employees were union. Even though North Carolina is a right-to-work state, the school system allowed staff to join a union; however, they did not officially recognize the union. Regardless, I took my role very seriously. I never had a problem with the union during my tenure.

During my public school employment, I started attending an educational program created by the International Executive Housekeeper Association (IEHA) at the local technical college with my peers. While this was not a degree credential program, the modules exposed me to different theories and models of leadership and management. I completed the program in 1995, passed the competency test, and became a Certified Executive Housekeeper (CEH). I was hungry for that kind of knowledge. I learned many of the theories that were being taught about management and leadership, much of which I had already been applying on the job. The courses affirmed for me that my supervisory skills were competent, but I realized I would need to go more in depth with my educational development to go beyond my supervisory role. I thought about going back to college then, but I still was not ready.

I really excelled in my role with the school system, but I quickly learned there was no room for growth. I looked outside of the school system, and after several application attempts with another local university, I was hired as the support administrator, my first mid-level management role in a PWI.

Leading to Change the World

We Were the Daughters

My daughter will be a warrior.
She will hunt and fish.
Learn how to gather and nurture,
all with a spoonful of my love.
I will raise her to be strong and proud.
I will teach her that self-love is preservation
And that only knowledge and wisdom will give you
salvation.
I will regard her as a goddess instead of my princess.
I will teach her the beauty of her spirit will take you
farther then a tight ass with loose hips or a fake weave and
liquid tips.
I will make sure she understands that love is freedom
And peace is a revolution of the soul.
I will assure her that tears can be a catharsis and not a
weakness, according to those who fear your power and want
to oppress your spirit
My daughter will be sharpened for battle.
And when the time comes, her eyes will be wide and alive
and full of the power she holds
From the way down-inside, all within the flowing rivers of
herself. She will take the world by storm,
And like her mother's possess the power
and the form of the wind.
My daughter will be a warrior.
Birthed from my womb with honor and sword in hand
With wisdom from those before her imprinted deep
within her palms
She will walk through a blood-tainted earth,
remembering hymns and psalms sung by women
who have broken their hips and backs in the name of
being strong.
My daughter will be a warrior.
Stronger and wiser with her-story based in the victory of
the silences I have battled,

Leslye Renee Kornegay, EdD

She will speak it, breathe, it, and live it knowing the
women before her
Took up space, allowing for the grace that is her to exist.
My daughter will be a warrior.[75]
By Windy Paz-Amor

Letter to My Mother:

Dear Mom,

I was the first of your children to permanently disfigure your body from childbirth. You were 24 years old when I was born, a military wife. While I do not remember a lot before the age of eighteen months, when my younger brother was born, I have heard stories of your courageous acts to protect your first-born over the years. There were two incidents in Florida that could have ended my life when I was a toddler. One involved you stomping a snake to death that had slithered up on the patio rail. It had its teeth ready to bite, but you came to check up on me just in time. Your mother's instinct kicked in, and without stopping to think about what kind of snake it was, you stomped that snake DEAD with your bare feet. Later, you learned it was venomous, and if it had bitten either of us, we would have died within five minutes.

Another time, when a venomous spider found me again in a similar predicament, you were there for me. I've often heard you tell those stories, and it always brings a smile to my face when you talk about protecting your baby. You have been the one constant in my life, and I am blessed to have you as my mother.

You have always stood on the side of what is just and instilled in me the values that I role model to this day. You taught me how to stand up for myself, simply through leading by example. I remember when we returned from Japan; in so many ways our experiences were beyond comprehension for a lot of people when we would talk about what we had done and what we had seen. People often thought we were making it up. They just could not imagine high speed lines underground moving faster than the speed of a bullet or cartoons with characters whose eyes were like saucers—characters that would eventually make their way into our US households. On one occasion when my younger brother was in the third grade and he had to do a show-and-tell presentation, you had worked with him to find some items to take to class depicting our travels in Japan, and he was so excited. During his presentation, he mentioned that the Tokyo Tower was the tallest building in the world at the time. He even had pictures and literature on it, but the teacher—a southern White woman teaching in an integrated public school—disregarded it all and called him a liar in front of the entire class. My brother burst into tears and came HOME very upset. When you found out about it, you left work early and went to see the principal, demanding to see him without an appointment. You explained to him what had happened, and he tried to side with the teacher, but you were not going to hear that. You said, "I READ him up, down, and sideways," and when you were finished with him, he was a *"done turkey!"* My brother never had another problem at that school.

Another time was when you went up to the high school because they had suspended my older step-brother. His girlfriend at the time had slapped him, and he slapped her back. They suspended him, but not his girlfriend, because they said boys should not hit girls. To you, that was not acceptable. Once again, you were fearless as you marched right up to that school and demanded to speak to the principal. You proceeded to tell them that you had taught all of your children that if someone hit us, we were to knock their asses out. "Don't let anyone mistreat you. You don't go out starting nothing, but you will finish it if you are provoked," you told us. "People need to know they cannot just disrespect you. If you let them, they will."

If they suspended him, they needed to suspend the girl too. You insisted that your step-son had acted in self-defense, and there were witnesses to attest. My step-brother was an all-American at the time, and he had never been in any kind of trouble like that. He was truly a gentleman. You informed the principal you would take the matter to the school board and beyond if you had to. The girl had six-inch nails that curved like cat claws. So, in addition to slapping your step-son, she had also clawed his very handsome face. You were fearless and courageous when it came to your children.

You never had to go to the school on my behalf. I was the "model child" who never got into trouble, except for when I got an F in geometry. Even then, you did not have to go up to the school on my behalf. I just wish that you had been better informed about what I would need to do early in my education to prepare me for life after high school—things like early preparation for college entrance tests, partnering me with mentors to help guide my educational choices, and sending me to camp or boarding school. I also wish you had been able to attend more of my extracurricular activities—gymnastics, track, basketball, cheerleading. I was a very strong athlete, and your active support could have influenced me to pursue these activities more seriously, maybe even as a profession beyond school. You never said it was not ladylike, or that there was no future in it (this was before Title VII of the Civil Rights Act) because you did let me participate.

In fairness to you, Mom, you held down a full-time job and were the primary HOME caretaker for a family of six—cleaning, cooking, and running the household. You did not have the time or the resources to fully support all of your children's interests. After all, my step-brother was the one we thought would have had a real future in sports. He would be the one who would need to support a family after school. At least that was still the norm in the early 1970s. I don't know where you would have found the time, but you were there for me in other ways as I developed into an adult.

You were and continue to be one of my strongest sources of support. Your actions spun the thread that bounds and grounds me as a human being. You taught me how to value others by respecting them for their inner beauty and not letting the outer shell of a person determine how I interact with them. You taught me how to accept people based upon their treatment of me versus judging them purely by differences like skin color. You taught me not to judge a book by its cover. Everyone has value and should be respected.

Mom, I always believed you were born ahead of your time. I know if you had been afforded the opportunity to go to college, you would have been the leader in whatever role you assumed. Others in your family and community look to your leadership; you have been a strong, courageous role model for me especially. You allowed me to find my path in this life and gave me continuous encouragement to break the mold as a Black woman by supporting my choice to pursue a career and not to take the normative path for women in our society. You did that for me. My journey has been filled with many twists and turns along the way. Whenever I would get discouraged and say I couldn't do something, you would always respond back with, "Who told you, you could not do that? There is only one being that can do that besides yourself and that is the Supreme being." You always said, "You will be your biggest barrier. If you think you cannot do something, chances are you probably will fail."

You were there to support me during all of my struggles and my path to reinventing myself to be the daughter and leader that I have become. Thank you for planting those warrior seeds for me at birth. Your guidance has prepared me to become the daughter you envisioned. While I now reside more than 700 miles from you, I will always carry the image of *HOME* you instilled in me as a child with me wherever I go in this life. I am proud to be your daughter, and I hope you continue to be proud of me.

Love always,
Your daughter,
Leslye

Leslye Renee Kornegay, EdD

Letter to Leslye from Daddy:

Dear Leslye (lez-sel-lee),

    I am writing you this letter because there are a number of things you should know. I wish I could have told you these things in person while I was living, but we do not choose how and when our lives will be taken. My death started the day I had my first stroke. That was followed by many strokes and finally my paralysis, leaving me immobile from the neck down. The last time I saw you, I was in the Veterans hospital in Virginia. You had traveled to see how I was doing. I know seeing me lying there, unable to move or even give you a hug or a kiss, was hard for you. I was rendered helpless when a fly decided to irritate me in your presence, and I remember you could not rest until you stopped that pest in its tracks. Just like when you were a child, you always fought to protect your Daddy, didn't you? Even when I did not deserve it.

    You were my first born, and I loved you more than I loved myself. When your mother divorced me, something in my spirit died as well. Yes, I guess I did become the kind of dad who just sent child support to justify their parentage. I failed to give you the quality time that you needed from me growing up. I hope you can forgive me for that. You turned out well in spite of me. Your mother and Mr. Mack deserve the credit for raising you; however, I never stopped loving you.

    Since I have been gone, I have watched you fulfill the goals you had set for yourself the last time I saw you. You have gone beyond those goals to have other successes in your life. I remember you standing there that day with tears streaming down your face. You did not want me to see you crying. If I could have, I would have hugged you and rocked the tears away the way I used to do when you were a child.

    While I could not smile, if you recall my eyes teared up, it was the only sign I could give you that I heard you and I was proud of you. I always knew you had strength and courage to fulfill your dreams even as a child, you were an old soul. You always had a mind of your own. I am not surprised that you have become a strong and viable leader. You have accomplished things in your life that other Black people and women still dream about.

You should be proud of your accomplishments. I understand you have now completed your doctoral degree, and I am so proud of you. I wish I could've been there to see you receive those honors in person, but don't worry, I was there in the spirit. Leslye, I hope that you can forgive me for any hurt or pain that I have caused you over the years. When you think of me, I hope you think of the good times we had during my time on earth. I will always be your dad, and I love you very much. Eternal love,
Dad

Chapter Four: Kornegay Journey to Director

My first mid-level management position in higher education was working in a large-scale housekeeping department at a PWI. I applied for a position at the state university three times before I was finally extended an interview and ultimately hired in 1995. I had heard it was difficult to get hired at the university level because there were so many applicants, so much competition; it seemed everyone wanted a state job. My grandmother, mother, and several other relatives worked for the state. I'd decided if it was good enough for them, it was good enough for me. Back then, state jobs were perceived as the kind of job you would have for the rest of your working life. The understanding at the time was that no one ever got fired from a state job unless they *really* messed up.

The university was really a small city in itself. When I was hired, it had around 35,000 students and 12,500 employees. Most of the Black employees worked in housekeeping. There were close to 400 housekeepers and, by my estimation, 99 percent of them were Black. My supervisor, the assistant director, was a Black man, and his assistant was a Black woman. I was hired to provide training support for the department and manage the calendar for all employee work assignments.

Two years after I started, my director retired. I applied for his job and so did his assistant, Sheila. We both made it to the interview stage of the search process. Sheila got the job. Later, several of the search committee members expressed that they had been very impressed with my interview. Before speaking to me, they had not realized there was another talent in the housekeeping department. Sheila was my first career role model. I really looked up to her. I thought, *Finally, I have someone who looks like me in a senior leadership role who can mentor me and help me become the leader I know I was meant to be.* Shortly after she began her new role, I requested a meeting with her to discuss my career plans.

I had started taking courses at the university, and two courses in my undergraduate program had really discouraged me from continuing my education. I knew if I wanted to progress in my professional field, I would have to do more than my peers to succeed. Not going back to school was not an option for me. I felt like anything was possible as long as I worked hard at it. That had been drilled into me at a young age. It was what my parents had taught me and what their parents had taught them.

Simply having a degree would not be enough, as I would later learn. What I know now is that a mentor could have helped guide me to develop the skills I needed to transition from a manager into a leader. Instead, I taught myself how to lead. According to Joseph Economy and Fonda Nelson, there are significant differences between the skill set needed to *manage* an organization and the skills required to *lead* an organization. In their book, *Managing Leadership for Dummies,* Economy and Nelson suggested:

> Managers are experts at taking their current organizations and optimizing them to accomplish their goals to complete their work. Managers focus on the here and now. Leaders differ in that they have vision. Leaders look beyond the here and now to see the vast potential of their organizations. Managers use policies, procedures, schedules, milestones, incentives, discipline, and other mechanisms to push their employees to achieve the goals of the organization. The threat of discipline or termination is always very real. Leaders differ in that they challenge their employees to achieve the goals of the organization by creating a compelling vision of the future and then unlocking their employee's potential.[76]

While managing operations and supervising people came naturally to me, I found myself unable to grow in my profession for a number of reasons. I kept hitting the proverbial glass ceiling, despite the fact that I was a model performer who always got outstanding and glowing reviews. It seemed opportunities were out of my reach because I did not have a formal education. I would later discover that in order for me to move from one role to another, I would need to once again reinvent myself and transform my self-taught mid-level manager skills into the skills required to be an effective leader. If I was committed to doing this work, I could not let others define my potential, and I had the will and the perseverance to go the distance. I had been a lifelong learner but had never finished my college degree due to a fear of failure. It was now time to conquer that fear and move on with the next phase of my life.

In March 1998, my father passed away. During the eulogy at his funeral, the pastor posed several questions to the congregation that challenged us to think about whether we had lived our lives in such a way that we knew what people would say about us when we pass away. I was reminded of my own vision quest and the unanswered questions that remained. When the pastor asked us what legacy we wanted to leave behind, I felt as if he was speaking directly to me. I still had a lot of work to do in my spiritual walk toward fully finding my purpose in life.

The eulogy at my father's funeral, *And, Then There Was Light...*, prompted a pivotal point in my life. It reinforced my vision quest, to determine what I wanted my legacy to be and what my contribution to the greater common good should look like. I was 40 years old. I was warned by my elders that I had inherited my father's health risk factors, and they motivated me to quit smoking. I knew that only then could I begin to live my best possible life.

The day I quit smoking was unplanned. I had been having problems with allergies and had been generally feeling bad for a while. I had read a number of books, not necessarily about quitting smoking, but motivational works about self-transformation, like *You Can Heal Your Life* by Louise Hay. Around that time, I also began daily walks with my sister. We would get up at five in the morning and walk five miles together, four or five days a week. During those nature walks, I found myself able to think about my life's purpose and what I wanted for myself. The walks were healing, calming, and spiritual for me; they helped me put things into better perspective.

So, even though my quit smoking day was not planned, the internal preparation had occurred over a course of several years. I had never tried to quit smoking before in the 26 years since I had picked up my first cigarette. I was afraid if I tried to quit and failed, that would make me a failure. There had never been anyone in my life who had role modeled a successful quit. My mom would stop smoking for a while but always picked up the habit again. My step-dad stopped for 17 years, but living with another smoker made it too difficult for him to stop entirely. It certainly did not help that we were all living in the tobacco capital of the United States.

The fear of failure had kept me hostage for 26 years, and the quitting process would require a life change. There were no guidebooks at the time, and I was not interested in going to Smokers Anonymous (I always had success figuring it out by myself) or following any of the smoking cessation programs, like chewing nicotine gum or wearing a nicotine patch. I had seen too many people still smoking while chewing nicotine gum. Some wore the nicotine patch, then took it off when they wanted to smoke. I knew that for me to quit, it would have to start from within. No patch or gum would keep me from a cigarette if I was not truly committed to stopping. I had to love myself enough to quit.

While I understood intellectually that smoking carried certain risk factors, I filed that information away somewhere in my subconscious because it was not a real threat to me then. But, one day, it finally caught up with me. I recall my dentist asking me during one of my visits if I smoked, which he had never asked before because I had masked it for so long. He went on to say that he'd noticed some minor gum recession, something usually seen in smokers.

"It's not bad yet," he said. "But if you continue to smoke, you will have some problems."

That wake-up call made me realize that I was a walking time bomb. All of a sudden, it came together for me that my smoking habit could damage my body. I started to research everything I could on smoking and the effects it could have on long-term smokers, and I did not like what I found. However, I learned some very promising news. If I stopped smoking successfully for 10 years, I could reverse my prognosis and even add years to my life. The longer I remained smoke-free, the stronger the chances were that I could eradicate any future smoking-related issues. Now, well over 27 years later, I have managed to remain smoke-free. While I am thankful that I quit when I did, I wish that I had loved myself enough as a teenager to quit back then. Kicking my smoking habit did not completely eliminate my health problems, however. I still had asthma and allergies, prompted in large part by my smoking history. This was further motivation for me to never pick up another cigarette again.

Back then, I thought that I had overcame the hardest obstacle I would ever face. Boy, was I wrong. It only strengthened me to be able to cope with the struggles and challenges that were to come.

After I quit smoking, I had a renewed confidence in what I could accomplish. I began to have dreams about my life and what was possible for me. Once, I came across a motivational statement by an unknown author that impacted me so much on a personal level that I printed it out and pasted it on my wall at work as a daily reminder. It went something like:

> Time is not like a bank where you can put money in and take it out whenever you want. Unlike a bank, we only have 24 hours given to us every day. If we do not use that time wisely, we lose it forever. We cannot bank time.

I realized I had to do something meaningful every day and that what I did with my time was only as valuable as I made it. I had been working on my bachelor's degrees in sociology and criminal justice at the university, and I was still employed there. The job felt like a natural fit for me, but it was time to change my academic path to match my career goals.

Confronting My Fears

The major reasons for me not completing my undergraduate degree the first time around were my social life, my fear of math, specifically algebra II and statistics, and my aversion to taking physical education (PE). I dreaded PE because swimming was required, and I had never even tried to learn because I was afraid of failing at it. Also, like many Black women, I did not like to get my hair wet because it ruined the hairdo. Unlike White women, Black women could never just wash their hair and go, at least not the Black women I knew. It took a lot of hair maintenance to keep our hair "presentable."

In the fall of 1997, I started taking classes again and enrolled in the dreaded algebra II class, ultimately passing with a B+, and went on to complete my undergraduate degree in record time. In the process, I realized that all of the skills and credentials that I had amassed over the years equated to the degree experience in large part. I was already a practitioner and I realized that I would need to continue my education and obtain a master's degree if I wanted to break the proverbial glass ceiling into senior leadership within a PWI.

Shattering That Damn Proverbial Cement Ceiling

For the master's tools will never dismantle the master's house.
They may allow us temporarily to beat him at his own game,
but they will never enable us to bring about genuine change.
And this fact is only threatening to those women who still
define the master's house as their only source of support.[77]
~Audre Lorde

Learning how to advocate for myself through self-efficacy did not happen overnight. This growth as a leader happened during a time in our history when women and Black people often were not in leadership roles, so the models in the workforce were most often White men. It was not unusual for Black leaders to assimilate into the dominant culture's leadership style, as I had done myself at one point. I often heard other Black people refer to Black leaders who looked out for "the man" in the workplace more than their own as "Uncle Toms." This usually applied to Black people who were fortunate enough to have entry-level and mid-level supervisory roles at PWIs. If an employee failed to follow an established attendance policy, it might lead to disciplinary action. As a supervisor, I have had to discipline staff for failing to follow protocol and not calling into work if they were unable to report to work and have been accused of being an Uncle Tom for this. They felt I should have made an exception for other Black people. So, following company policy was perceived as me putting the company above my own race. These kinds of accusations occurred frequently.

My experience with employees working in these organizations during those times was that they did not have a sense of vested ownership; they did not believe the organizations valued nor cared about them as human beings. The organizations were not perceived as being very people-friendly. They relied on systems and policies to guide the process—rather than valuing their employees. In my earlier career, an employee's honest feedback could mean termination. This was typical in non-democratic workplaces, which relied on traditional management and leadership styles in the 1980s and 1990s. Employees were to be seen and not heard.[78] The employees had a point about the organizations not caring for them as people.

One policy that was not employee friendly related to inclement weather. The accumulation of snow in the South cannot compare to a typical Northern winter. However, because snow and ice occurrences are not regular events, when they do happen, there can be total chaos. The systems in place to support snow removal in the South are not as aggressive as they are in the North. Two inches of snow can create gridlock. Needless to say, organizations like a university with thousands of students required people in critical roles to report to work. Our snow policy mandated all critical role personnel, including housekeepers, to report to work. If an employee failed to report to work, they would be disciplined. Calling in to say you could not make it to work was also not acceptable.

During one of the worst ice storms that I can remember, one of our employees felt that he had no choice but to report to work on the night shift. He was a very young man with a wife and five kids, and he needed to keep his job. So, he got on the road, but he never made it to work. He had an accident that left him paralyzed from the neck down. Because the accident happened on his way to work, it was not considered job-related. The only support he received was from some employees within our department helping him, independent of the university. Eventually, he was able to secure disability benefits, but it was after at least a year of his family not receiving anything. To my knowledge, the university never publicly accepted any responsibility for what happened. Although the employee was committed to the organization, the organization was not committed to him and his family. Employee morale went down throughout the division, not just in housekeeping.

This incident strengthened my desire to continue my leadership growth. It was clearly a social justice issue that had been pushed aside. I had a real problem with this because it went against my values and my beliefs, but I was not in a position or a safe place to be able to advocate for this employee. So, I focused on excelling in nontraditional jobs for women, such as facilities, custodial management, and various leadership roles. There was a transitional period in which I had to develop the skills that worked best for me in order to be a successful leader. My ability to adapt to change was one of the characteristics that enabled me to serve as a transformational change agent several times in my career. As an agent of change, I successfully implemented full department reorganizations.

Gatekeepers

In my professional journey, I have encountered a number of gatekeepers, all of whom have impacted my career and motivated me to take charge of my own self-development. While I can draw upon a number of poor leadership examples, I also recall three individuals who motivated me to lead by example. Though they caused an uncomfortable emotional reaction in me that I have not experienced very often, I channeled that anger into doing something positive for myself. One of the individuals was a Black woman who advocated for my university hire in 1995, another was a former director who I worked with for more than eight years, and the third was my former director's boss. I had some pretty poor role models, but

I learned later in my journey that I could reach out to people outside my professional circle for advice.

In 1997, when I enrolled in the university to pursue my bachelor's degree, I was on a natural high. I had experienced my first string of successful outcomes, and the fear of failure was becoming a distant memory, so I set up an appointment with my assistant director to express my interest. Never in the history of this PWI had a Black woman been hired into the role of assistant director or director in the Finance and Business division.

Interestingly, I have only had one Black woman director in my entire career. I thought we had a lot in common, particularly because we were both Black women who had come up through the ranks at PWIs. In our shared experiences, we'd encountered similar obstacles, barriers, gatekeepers, and glass-ceiling experiences. I looked up to her as someone who had reached a level in her profession that I aspired to, and I really believed if I applied myself and demonstrated my strong work ethic, she would be open to mentoring me on a formal basis.

My meeting with Sheila took place shortly after I had quit smoking and resumed taking university courses. Even though I thought we had a pretty good relationship, I anxiously, hesitantly approached her office, knowing that I would be exposing my innermost thoughts to her by disclosing my future aspirations. After all, I considered her to be a role model and envisioned myself following in her footsteps one day. This meeting was so different from the social outings that we would often go on during our lunch breaks.

During our meeting, I shared that I had finally decided to take that dreaded algebra class that had kept me from pursuing my educational goals in the past. I wanted her to know that I could finally see the light at the end of the tunnel, which held my bachelor's degree at the other end. I explained to her that I wanted to discuss my career goals, and I wanted her to work with me to develop a plan to accomplish my goals. I will never forget her response.

"This is going to be hard," she said. "While I think going back to school is commendable and you should be proud of your accomplishments, I do not think it will be enough for you to grow beyond where you are currently at in this work environment."

Time stood still. Less than a minute had passed, yet it felt like an eternity. I literally ran out of her office, or at least it felt like I did. I guess I was afraid of her saying anything else. She shattered my spirit when she uttered those words. It was devastating to know that my role model could not see me ever leading an organization.

Thoughts raced through my mind. I admired and looked up to her, and she was two years younger than me for Pete's sake! The only difference that I could see between her and me was that she already had a bachelor's degree and I was still working towards getting mine. I was really hurt that she thought so little of my abilities. I wondered if she really felt that I was not capable of achieving what she had achieved. Or if she felt she was special because both of her parents were professors at Black colleges, well-known within the academic community. Or did she want to be the only Black woman in this kind of role at the institution?

Even though she did not seem to believe that I could reach my stated goals, I would not let her beliefs define my success. It seemed my new supervisor still viewed me as her competition. I had been naive to think that our sisterhood meant something to her. Once again, Audre Lorde's words resonated with me:

> Until now, there has been little that taught us how
> to be kind to each other. To the rest of the world,
> yes, but not to ourselves. There have been few
> external examples of how to treat another Black
> woman with kindness, deference, tenderness, or an
> appreciative smile in passing, just because she IS; an
> understanding of each other's shortcoming because
> we have been somewhere close to that, ourselves.
> When last did you compliment another sister,
> give recognition to her specialness? We have to
> consciously study how to be tender with each other
> until it becomes a habit because what was native
> has been stolen from us, the love of Black women
> for each other.[79]

By this point, I had already had many successes, such as quitting smoking and going back to college. I felt like I could accomplish anything that I set my mind to. Even before I quit smoking and continued my educational journey, I believed what my parents had been taught: Upward mobility could happen if I applied myself. Years later, in my doctoral program I would learn that most of my classmates had come into the program with social capital that I had been denied as a Black woman. Hard work alone does not guarantee success for people like me. There will be obstacles and barriers to overcome, and I would have to learn how to navigate my way around them throughout my personal and professional journey.

Interestingly, my experience aligned with that of the young Black men in Jay McLeod's study. Many of those young men believed if they worked hard, anything was possible.[80] I had thought the same thing. Surely, having a degree meant instant social upward mobility. Having a degree should mean I will be able to break the proverbial glass ceiling, right? I had always assumed that the only thing that had kept me from ascending into leadership was not having my undergraduate degree. The reality was much more insidious. The intersection of race, gender, and assigned sex (gender determined at birth) had a lot to do with my inability to grow in my profession. My experiences were similar to what other Black women have written about, stemming from the teachings passed down by strong Black women who raised them. Terri Hurdle shared her experience as a Black woman faculty member working in a PWI.

> If you endure until the end, you shall receive your reward. Even though the aforementioned states are true, my grandmother left out one component; they come with a price. The price can be in the form of lost relationships, taking on the responsibility of family members, or redirecting your dreams. It seems as if every opportunity slips through your fingers and the imaginary glass ceiling begins to close in on you. Suddenly, the confidence that was once personified in your stance starts to fade, as a result, your faith is shaken and just before you begin to break, you look for direction.[81]

It is not that I thought racism did not exist or that women did not always have a voice in our society. I had experienced the "-isms" before, but this was the 20th century. My ancestors were strong Black women, my SHEROs who had challenged society in their lifetime, fighting back during the civil rights and women's rights movements. I have always believed that I was born during the right time in history.

If it is true that babies picked their parents, then I have selected well to have chosen my mother. It has amazed me how strong Black women like her and my grandma Ninny managed their households, reared children, and still worked full-time jobs. They were leaders in their own time and really set the bar for me to rise to another level.

When I was growing up, clothes were hung up on the clothesline because there were no electrical clothes dryers. Food was grown in the family garden, pickled and canned, not bought in a grocery store. These women had to do all of these things. There were no fast food restaurants or hired hands to do the work for them. So, why could I not find women like Ninny and my mom in the workplace when I first started my career? Where were the women who looked at life like me and shared similar experiences to my own?

I had chosen to go into a profession where leadership roles were dominated by White men, a world very few women and Blacks have accessed even in the 21st century. Still, I could not understand why my attempts to grow in my profession were not being given serious consideration. Had I not worked my way up from the ground-level as a housekeeper in Atlantic City? I had come a long way in my career trajectory.

The glass ceiling had evolved into a cement ceiling for me— at least I had a view with a glass ceiling. A cement ceiling blocked my view to the privileges that I had been denied. I experienced the dripping motionless water feeling of taking control of my life. I realized that all of the gifts my mom, Ninny, and aunties had passed on to me were not valued in my workplace. My mother had planted seeds when I was born. She helped to pave the way for me to reach heights personally and professionally that she could not reach herself. Although my mother never frowned upon my choice of profession, she would provide gentle hints like, "If you went back to school, you could become a lawyer or something like that."

Don't get me wrong. I never believed my destiny was to be a leader in housekeeping. In fact, I worked very hard to get out of the housekeeping profession earlier in my career. After all, no one in my family had gone into that profession. I had been taught housekeeping was the work the house slave did for the master during slavery--not the kind of work that one could be proud of even today when the word "housekeeping" was mentioned to people who knew nothing about my profession, an image of a janitor sitting by a stove shoveling coals into the flame emerged? I would spend my professional career trying to create a more dignified image of the housekeeping profession and remove the stigma of plantations and slavery through my involvement with professional Environmental Service (we have evolved from housekeeping) associations years later.

Discovering My Voice

I soon learned that as a Black woman I would need to have more credentials than my peers when I applied for the same positions. So, immediately after completing my bachelor's degree, I enrolled in a graduate program. There, I was exposed to additional management and leadership theories beyond what I had learned in my bachelor's and certification program, Professional Association Management. Interestedly, I learned that many of the models and theories were not new to me. I was already performing at that level, I just did not have names for them. But it soon became clear that the unique problems I was experiencing as a Black woman in a profession dominated by White men were virtually invisible in the literature. I also came to understand that my transformational leadership style was a valuable asset because I had led numerous successful change initiatives and always left an organization much better off than when I started. In fact, I commonly visited organizations that I helped to build and found a viable staff of long-term employees still working there—people who I helped to hire, coach, and mentor in their professional development. I had never had a mentor take that kind of interest in my professional development, but through my self-taught skills, I was able to become that resource for my direct reports.

The incident I'd had with my former supervisor, Sheila, left me more determined than ever to succeed as a leader. Eventually, I would have a conversation similar to the one I'd had with her with the assistant director who replaced her. In 1985, he was the first Black man to ever be hired at the institution. When I think of him—old terms like "house slave" and "field slave" come to mind--not because of how I felt about him, but rather because of how I think he felt about *himself* and because of what I had heard people from all levels of the institution say about him.

Tom came from the pre-civil rights era commonly referred to in my community as the "old school" where a Black man did not challenge a White person under any circumstances, even if they had rights on their side. His work ethic reflected this belief, and I knew very early in his tenure that if he would not practice self efficacy and advocate for himself, he would not advocate for my staff or for me.

By the time Tom took over, I had nearly completed my master's degree. I had led a significant change initiative, which resulted in a promotion for me into a job that I designed for myself. This was my senior leadership role. Being the second Black woman to ever reach a senior role in our division and the first to ever hold this position brought with it some additional responsibilities that I was not prepared for. Being the *only* Black woman meant I was invited to sit on every search committee and every working group. I was also designated as an official spokesperson, expected to represent and advocate on behalf of all Black people in our division. This, of course, put unrealistic demands on me, but I persevered because to do otherwise would have meant no one representing Black people at those decision-making tables at all. That would become a familiar expectation in the future.

Once again, I took a chance and decided to share my career aspirations with my supervisor, Tom. During the annual employee performance review, a meeting where we also set future goals, I had a heart-to-heart discussion about my career goals. Tom acknowledged that I had done an outstanding job that year, yet he failed to recognize my outstanding work when he rated my performance. In response to his ratings, I took the initiative to outline all of the accomplishments that I made during the year. In most of the categories, I had exceeded performance expectations. I will never forget what he said to me, "I never give out outstanding ratings, because that would mean that someone was perfect." Later, when Tom hired a Black man who I had to train to take over my role, Tom gave him all outstanding evaluations during his first evaluation cycle. That was insecurity at its best. I really ran the department, and everyone knew it.

Tom began his career as a division head senior administrator, but he had been reassigned from one department to another over the years because he was an incompetent leader. We were all worse off when he ended up in housekeeping. He once told me, "I am sure when you finish your graduate degree you might decide to take up something in real estate to support the brokers licenses that you have. I think you would do very well in that kind of role."

> After all of the aforementioned blockades and barriers constructed by white, male gatekeepers, the wrath of cultural imperialism assumed an even more insidious form, as her grinnng "blackface" spouted the dialectical advantages of whiteface paradigms and cultural values. Many "race traitors" occupy professional positions and postures to accommodate institutional tyranny.[82]

This passage resonates with the very essence of my feelings about what happened to me. Even though this passage was directed at a Black woman who was Melba Byrd's former supervisor in her college, who attacked her work publicly to the dominant group because she felt Byrd presented a competitive threat, it still had a familiar ring to me. I believe Byrd's message is transferrable to Black men who fit this mold and act as gatekeepers for Black women in the university (academy).

When Tom made his comment about me going into real estate, I knew he would never see me as his equal. Less than a year later, he hired a Black man and began grooming him to take over the leadership role. My peer came into his role with no experience in the profession, and I realized once again that I would need to advocate for myself. All I wanted was for Tom to acknowledge my potential and mentor me like he did my new peer. That never happened.

Three years later, at the same institution, another conversation had a major impact on me that would set the course for me to look beyond the university for career advancement (another pivotal point). My director's boss (a White man) implemented a work practice to meet with all division leaders annually. During a meeting with him, he acknowledged my educational accomplishments and asked me what my goals were for the future. I shared with him that I wanted to be in his position one day. He never batted an eyelash or even verbally acknowledged what I had said to him. His facial expression told me everything I needed to know. He never directly responded to my career goals. When I left that meeting, I knew I would never be given the opportunity to grow under his leadership.

Like Sojourner Truth, I Was Northern Bound

In 2005, I left the State University system. I had to leave my family and HOME to grow professionally, to realize my dreams. My former institution was unable to find a successor to retain my former position for several years. That was not surprising because I had been the first person to serve in this role, and I had written the job description myself. It was the perfect job for me at that time; however, it offered no upward mobility. That's why my decision to leave felt right. Sometimes you have to leave a position to grow. Less than three years after I left the university in North Carolina, I realized my dream of becoming a director of custodial services at a PWI, a well-respected public Ivy League university.

Shortly after I became the director, Sheila, my former director, who had told me there was a glass ceiling and she could not see me going any further, contacted me.

Several years after my devastating conversation with Sheila, she resigned from the institution and went into business for herself. She emailed me to explain that her business accounts were not going well, and she was exploring career options, even considering going back into higher education. Sheila said that my feedback was valuable to her, and she admired the growth that I had achieved as a leader. In addition, she wanted me to review her resumé and asked if I would provide a recommendation for her.

"You have gone much further in the profession than I ever did," she said.

I was floored. The woman who had devastated me, a decade later, was giving me accolades for going beyond anything she had ever accomplished. That was totally contrary to what she told me when I was struggling to grow. I am so grateful that I did not let her take away my spirit to do the work I was called to do. Life provided the most unexpected twists and turns.

Shattering That Damn Proverbial Glass Ceiling All Over Again

It is clear to me now that the role that I was in at the time determined the leadership style that I performed. My first exposure to leadership was traditional in nature, which was hierarchical and paternalistic, as opposed to the flat organizational structure I adopted later in my career, servant and organic leadership.[83] During a transitional period, I had to develop the skills that worked best for me to be a successful leader. My ability to adapt to change was one of the characteristics that enabled me to serve as a transformational change agent three distinct times in my career and successfully implement full department reorganizations.

During the recruitment for the director of custodial services, the institution recruited me based on my demonstrated experience as a change agent who had led a diverse staff. I was aggressively recruited by the university and ultimately accepted my first senior level position in higher education in 2007. Within 10 years, I had grown from an entry-level supervisor at a major university in the South into an executive leadership role for a well-respected public Ivy League institution. I was the first Black woman hired in a senior-level role for my division. For many years, I remained the only Black woman at this level in my division. I managed a newly merged department of more than 200 employees, consisting of people from 20 different countries, speaking 21 different languages. They were some of the lowest paid employees on campus, represented by the United Workers of America.

I had been drawn there because of the diverse staff of employees in the department and the fact that the university had been proactive in the areas of social justice and diversity, but there was still much work to be done in these areas. The university embodied the kind of employer characteristics that I had been searching for in my career. I felt that I was at the right place at the right time to be able to give back to the group of employees who needed me the most. Being in this role, my social justice, equity, and ethical leadership skills were refined by applying what I had learned in my educational studies and through practical experience I had developed as a leader. In 2007, I made the decision to return to my first love, working with the most marginalized group in my profession, the housekeepers. Having gone from an Atlantic City housekeeper early in my career to the role of director, I could not only talk the talk, but I could walk the walk. I had instant credibility with the housekeepers. I was the voice for the department, and I advocated for my employees.

Sustaining in the Late 2000s Financial Crisis

In 2008, the university, much like the rest of the world, experienced an economic downfall similar to the Great Depression. Millions of people were out of work. The university experienced a $25 million shortfall, which impacted my department. Because my budget was mostly made up of human capital, I had to strategically plan my budget reduction proposal to manage my department's share of the deficit. My goal was to save as many filled positions as possible. Working with my leadership team, we reduced cleaning tasks and frequencies for all private spaces in university buildings from five days a week to one day a week and gave the responsibility of waste removal in private offices to the office occupants. We provided the office occupants with a desktop mini trash bin that they could empty out in a designated public receptacle in their buildings. The housekeepers then only had to remove the waste from the public spaces to the dumpsters.

This single service level change related to 3,000 offices and reduced the number of laborers to support this task by 10 positions, which were eliminated through attrition so no employees were laid off. At the time, it seemed simple to implement because I had led that kind of change before in North Carolina. However, in the history of the institution, service frequencies had never been adjusted. Staff and faculty were in an uproar in response to the news that their offices would no longer be cleaned daily. The service level changes did not impact our student areas on campus because the main focus of the service change was to reduce services in spaces that were not student-centered. Administrative offices do not directly impact the student experience. Somehow people lost sight of why they worked for the university.

What began as a simple implementation took courage to follow because while senior administration realized the real need driving this change, no one wanted to deal with their own staff when they complained about the need for the change. I realized to make this change work, I had to advocate on custodial service's behalf. I did this by presenting the new housekeeping model to the campus community with informational sessions, which gave departments the opportunity to ask questions regarding how the change would affect them. The outcome was a win for my department and the university at large.

The services we provided were in line with our peer institutions. I had a vision of what a world-class housekeeping department should look like, and it became a shared vision, which led to the department becoming the model for other custodial departments.[84] A number of institutions have changed their waste removal and service reductions based on our model. I did a number of interviews with universities and external media to communicate how I was able to manage the custodial budget shortfall and change initiative.

As a leader, I learned very early in my career that building trust and confidence with your staff is necessary for effectiveness. That trust takes time to build and can be destroyed in a second.[85] Being straightforward comes easy when you have earned the respect of your staff. I believe out of all the traits a leader can possess, the single most important trait is integrity. Additionally, a leader must be a moral person as well as a moral manager; it is a characteristic that should be the whole person, not the role that you are in at the time.[86] Being anything other than an ethical leader has never been an option for me.

When I first began my leadership journey, I recall not having a guidebook for ethical leadership. My success came from the values and beliefs that were instilled in me during my childhood. My smelling sense (using my intuition to shift through something to gain an understanding) and those earlier experiences would kick in when it came to leadership and how I dealt with dilemmas in the workplace. On a scholarly level, I drew from a number of ethical platforms and paradigms to assist me with my ethical decision-making. I employed concepts from ethical theorists in the areas of justice, care, profession, and critique. I was able to follow Lipmen-Blumen's[87] connective leadership model to construct a visual constellation of my leadership style during those times. My strong character preferences were identified as *Direct*: power, intrinsic, and competitive, 28 percent; *Relational*: contributory, collaboration, and vicarious, 35 percent; and finally *Instrumental*: personal, social, and entrusting 32 percent. At that time, my constellation reading indicated a balanced tendency in my leadership approach.

Depending upon a given situation, I would adjust my leadership approach to respond appropriately.[88] That proved to be a powerful tool for my leadership development. It enabled me to view my leadership style through the perspective of others, to better understand how my leadership style was learned, and to seek new holistic ways to approach leadership on a continual basis.

Leslye Renee Kornegay, EdD

I recall a conversation I once had with a Black woman in senior leadership whom I admired. She talked about some of the dilemmas she had faced as a woman of color in higher education and how her values and beliefs were challenged during those times. She talked about how she was able to grow and lead in a very political environment. Little did I know that interview would lead to my first autoethnographic pilot study in my doctoral program. This initial conversation was one of the early "Aha" moments for me, the realization that my leadership trajectory could be a focus of my doctoral research (another pivotal moment). I had certainly had my share of dilemmas, challenges, obstacles, barriers, and successes while in leadership roles at PWIs.

My journey to New England brought about different challenges for me than what I had experienced in the South. The challenges I encountered in the South had centered around the intersection of race, class, gender, and assigned sex. In the South, a good old boy would tell you upfront, "I don't like you, but I'll work with you." You had arrived if your income enabled you to buy a HOME beside them. Money had no color. Southern people are very pleasant, and you might hear "hello" and "how are you" from all kinds of people. In that type of environment, I knew what I was dealing with.

In the North, I found it to be vastly different. During the three years I lived and worked up north, the challenges I faced were not as much about race as they were about ethnic groups, sexual orientation, and gender.

An example of this is the race classification of Cape Verdeans, which is Portuguese intermingled with other races. This classification only exists on official documentation in Massachusetts because there is a very high concentration of that population in the state. While I was in Massachusetts from 2005 to 2007, my first career move outside of North Carolina, I observed many Cape Verdeans self-disclose as White, Black, Portuguese, or Cape Verdean on employee applications, especially those who resided outside the Commonwealth of Massachusetts. The environment was extremely unionized, which added another layer to the dynamics. North Carolina was a right-to-work state, which meant unions could be formed but the state did not officially recognize unions in negotiations.

In *Shifting: The Double Lives of Black Women in America*, Jones and Shorter-Gooden wrote,

> Shifting is often internal, invisible. It's the chipping away at her sense of self, at her feelings of wholeness and centeredness—often a consequence of living amidst racial and gender bias.[89]

From 2007 to 2016, I lived in Vermont, having been recruited and promoted as the inaugural Director of Custodial Services at the University of Vermont. Vermont was different from both North Carolina and Massachusetts. I found Vermont to be a very White state with much work to do in the area of race, ethnicity, gender, and class. On the surface, people were sociable, but not overly so in the beginning. I have found that Northerners, on average, take about two years to warm up to outsiders; if you survive, then you might get a "hello."

I found that building relationships outside of the university community was challenging. Even within the university, I quickly learned that people had their own little cliques and silos. Many of the people who looked like me did not venture outside of their circles frequently. I would later learn some of them had been burned by members of the dominant group, and, as a protective measure, they did not get too close to people outside of their circles. There were a lot of long-term staff and faculty, and the assumption was if you were a transplanted newcomer, chances were you would only be at the university for a little while.

It is hard building relationships in that kind of environment. I quickly learned that I had to keep my associations private. Once again, I drew very heavily upon my skills and ability to adapt in two worlds I learned as a child to adjust—to "shift"— in my new White surroundings. I made it a point to spend the first three months in my new role as director introducing myself and networking with as many campus community members as I could.

After my honeymoon period on the job, I quickly ascertained that what had at first appeared to be a very inclusive, diverse climate during my interview was far from what I initially envisioned. The university had a lot of work to do in the area of diversity and inclusion for its staff, students, and faculty. I knew immediately that if I was going to be successful in this environment, I would need to call out and name any racist interactions with members of the dominant group. My experiences had taught me that if you allow it to happen one time without addressing it, it will happen again.

One of the first racist incidents I encountered in Vermont occurred shortly after I had begun working at the institution. My arrival had not caught up with the housekeeping kinds of support functions that typically go along with a new hire. As director, I had to rely on my staff to make appointments for me because my employee access to the corporate calendar was still in the queue. I had committed myself to meet all of my key business partners. Somehow, the timing of one of my appointments was off by 30 minutes. This was my first meeting with Peggy, a White woman who had been at the institution for a number of years and held a very prominent role within my division.

When I arrived for my appointment thinking that I was on time, I noticed that she did not get up to greet me. She was cold, distant, and unsmiling. In a very sour, hateful tone, she said, "Around here, we have something called our common ground. We respect each other's time. We do not arrive at meetings late." I knew she had a chip on her shoulder by her tone and the fact that she still had not looked at me to acknowledge my presence. I was insulted, embarrassed, and reminded of the stereotype that is synonymous with Black folk—that we are unprofessional and always late. I remember thinking to myself, *Okay, it is not your fault that you were late. Regardless, take the high road and do not let her ignorance make you look bad by cussing her out.* Although, if I had gotten mad, it would have been an opportunity to madvocate.

Robert Nash describes the madvocate—one of five communication strategies for social justice advocate—as someone who "teaches through anger, righteous indignation, and moral outrage."[90] While the context of using this strategy had a student-centered approach to social justice, I have found it is very useful when managing social advocacy conflicts with adults. I got through that very unpleasant meeting, then took some time to process what had happened. I really did not want to attribute it to negative stereotypes about my race, but I also knew that her behavior toward me had been unprofessional. So, I decided to bring my concerns to my supervisor. Upon hearing my story, he proceeded to tell me that he had known Peggy for years and he had never heard anyone complain about this kind of behavior from her before. This just was not like Peggy, he said and surmised that maybe something else was going on with her.

I was not surprised by his response, a dismissal of my concerns as a Black woman. It was, after all, the typical White person's response to a Black person naming a racist act. *My perception of what happened is what validated the action, not his.* I think, in some part, he tried to minimize what had happened to protect me as the first Black person to lead in the organization. I suspect I was the first Black woman Peggy had been forced to interact with on the job. He later told me that he did talk to her about the incident, but she never apologized. Interestingly, she would go on to assist me with developing programming for my department. Several years later, she retired, and every time I called to request consulting work, she accepted without hesitation. Even though I did not get a verbal apology from her, I was still able to take the higher road— known as the "gladvocacy" social justice approach. To do less would have played into the Angry Black Woman stereotype that paints Black women as threatening and aggressive.

One time, as I was entering a campus building, the solid door swung open to reveal a White woman on the other side, exiting through the same door. I guess she was not prepared to see me and had not been able to put her mask on yet because she screamed when she saw me. I saw the raw fear on this woman's face, her blatant racism.

Are you kidding me? I thought.

Throughout my career, I have performed activities that have enabled me to sustain my leadership performance. I have practiced self-efficacy as a Black woman. I actively insisted on professional development for my leadership team and for me. Among other things, I attended Stephen Covey's Seven Habits workshop and completed a 360-degree survey on my leadership style to identify areas that needed additional development. I have used emotional intelligence instruments that have benefited me in developing my leadership style and the people who I have mentored into leadership who continue to lead with caring and compassion.[91] Research has shown emotional intelligence can have a direct impact on the development of resonant leaders.[92]

All of my direct reports at the University of Vermont also took the Myers-Briggs Personality Inventory. This proved invaluable for matching team members with tasks that aligned with their natural tendencies so they could be successful, and it also helped with peer understanding of each other's personality types.

It has been my experience that organizations rise only as high as their leadership. If the leadership is poor, the organization will perform poorly; if the leadership is excellent, the organization will excel.[93] Some of the leaders interviewed in the book *Leading Coherently* highlighted the dispositions of high-performing leaders. For example, being centered, analytic, relative, positive, persistent, curious, and invested influence leadership sustainability.[94]

Experience has taught me that having a vision, direction, and plan as a leader is important. When I look back, I can truly say I have had only one leader who fit this mold. Too often, people have arrived in positions of leadership and failed because they had no direction. This was very true in my early years when promotions happened through favoritism and entitlement. In spite of these early examples of poor leadership, I worked very hard when I became a leader to promote employees based on competencies, such as education, cultural diversity, knowledge, skills, and work experience.

As a leader, I found it very beneficial to create a shared vision, mission, and core value statement with the other leaders in my department. This helped to foster inclusion and understanding of the department's mission in the absence of a clear directive. I have found that it helped to give the staff a sense of pride and empowerment, as well as confidence that their roles are important to the institution. Working with my leaders and staff, we developed a set of core values with the acronym "I CARE": Integrity, Communication, Respect, and Excellence.

My department's vision was in line with the institutional vision and mission. From that shared vision came the shared development of strategic goals to set the vision into a planned course of action. My department has been very successful with aligning the department's mission to the university's mission, as we achieved with the budget reduction and service level changes. This also aligned with student and staff quality of life within the department.

I have always believed that a good leader helps to develop their staff by setting an example for their managers and staff to emulate. As a leader who knows what it is like not to have a mentor, I have taken the initiative to mentor my staff members who have demonstrated growth potential, the ones who stood above the rest in performance. I worked with their strengths and provided them the tools they needed to become successful leaders. My own experience of not having a formal mentor drove my need to mentor new leaders and help them to realize their potential. Following my example, I had staff continue to complete their degrees and go on to become leaders themselves. Some of them have gone further into their career track, while others have pursued other passions. Many of the high performers I mentored over the years developed their skills enough to assume my role after I left an institution.

A good leader plans to leave their organization in better shape than it was when they arrived. They also need to be able to make difficult decisions when necessary, while continuously seeking out new and innovative ways to make change and achieve continuous improvement. I have always encouraged my staff members to think outside the box and to view challenges as opportunities. I have led using a leadership style that draws from the visionary, servant, transformational, collaborative, and organic styles. While I have always encouraged team members to provide input regarding decisions that impact the entire team, when we could not come to a consensus, I made the hard decisions. However, throughout my trajectory, it has become increasingly clear to me that, as a Black woman leading in a PWI, any authority I have is borrowed. When the chips fly, all of that authority goes out the window.

In my experience, the more responsibility you have as a leader, the less power you actually have because your success is really dependent upon the success of the employees you lead. In his book, *Principle-Centered Leadership,* Stephen Covey describes three types of power for leaders: coercive, utility, and principlecentered.[95] I have embraced the principle-centered leadership style the most. This leadership style is rooted in care and a sincere belief in my employees and in what they are trying to accomplish. The employees of this type of leader trust, respect, and honor their leadership because the leader is actually a servant of the employee, not vice versa. It's interesting to me that I have reached such incredible milestones in my career and I still find myself in a servant role.

This emerging approach to leadership and service is called servant leadership. Servant leadership is a unique form of leadership that is crucial to a language-learning type of organizational change. Servant leadership holds that profit is not the primary purpose of a business; instead, it is to create a positive impact on its employees and community.[96] The nine characteristics that help servant leaders transform organizations are:

- Their ability to listen and empathize with others
- Understanding the need to help heal those who have broken spirits or feel disenfranchised
- Being aware of their own strengths and weaknesses
- Being aware of the strengths and weaknesses of the members of their organization
- Their reliance on the art of persuasion
- Ability to conceptualize
- Ability to foresee the likely outcomes of situations and decisions
- Stewardship and commitment to the growth of people
- Being dedicated to building community

In "The Leadership Styles and Practice of University Women in Administrative Presidencies," a study conducted by A. Maitra, the researcher sought to discover some of the factors that have contributed to the success of women leaders on campus. The researcher focused on the following areas: (1) the perceptions of current women vice presidents in nonacademic roles regarding leadership styles and practices they use to lead their functional areas, (2) the impact of their educational, professional, and personal backgrounds on their success, and (3) the perception of current women vice presidents about the road to successful leadership as advisable to future women leaders on campus. The research methods that were used in this study include Bolman-Deal's Leadership Orientations Survey (SELF) and Kouzes and Posner's Leadership Practice—Inventory (LPI - SELF). Both were used to collect information on the participants' leadership styles and practices.[97]

The results showed that women vice presidents used a multi-frame leadership orientation in their leadership styles; scored highest in the human resource frame followed by structural, symbolic, and political frames; and led by the leadership practice of enabling others to act followed by modeling the way, encouraging the heart, challenging the process, and inspiring a shared vision. These findings add to the growing body of research in the area of leadership styles of women in higher education administration.

In another study, J.M. Gaetane explored Black women in higher education administration through the lens of transformational leadership, social change, core values, empowering others, United States mentality, leader not being dominant, and shared inquiry and solution.[98] The most significant points I gleaned from this paper were that a good leader demonstrates a selfless desire to both serve and prepare others and creates an organizational system that is committed to developing and sharing relationships that drive visions.

In an article titled "How Salsa, Soul, and Spirit Strengthen Leadership," Juana Bordas suggests that there is an organic paradigm at work, with a multicultural focus on inclusion. The organic paradigm consisting of leadership practices—

incorporating values, respect, and potential encouragement and engagement—were all characteristic of women of color in leadership positions. Furthermore, their leadership practices included a mosaic world centered on listening to servanthood, vision, spirituality, partnership, kinship, community of leaders, practices, vision networks, and culturally effective community. Bordas argued that there is a need for leaders to embrace all of the characteristics in order to be good leaders, and in doing so these leaders are able to create a safe work environment. Leadership styles were presented as community-based in nature, with a spiritual connection of gratitude and graciousness—all characteristic of women of color.[99]

While I have had many successes as a leader throughout my trajectory, I have also encountered attacks on my leadership due to my race and assigned sex. I have shared a number of stories in my professional journey that speak to the evil that I have encountered in the workplace at the hands of my supervisors and colleagues while working in PWIs. Sustaining and navigating my leadership during challenging times has been a work in progress for me. There is certainly evil everywhere in our society, but I had never encountered such evil in the workplace until I journeyed North.

When I arrived in the North in 2005, as a new executive, I was pretty naive. I assumed if someone was in a leadership role, it was because the institution recognized them as a competent, ethical leader. We all have values and beliefs that help to make up who we are. However, in the workplace, ethical behavior should be expected as a matter of common ground practices that all adhere to. In my experience in higher education, this has not been the case.

There is a plethora of literature regarding ethics and morality in the workplace. Researcher A. Beerel investigated the hypothesis that the power dynamics inherent in business corporations and a culture of fear constituted important factors that contributed to the gap between ethical theory and moral behavior in business practice.[100] Examining the ethics-morality gap in the business domain had not been approached prior to this study.

Previous studies focused on the ethical intentions of business people and whether women conceptualize ethical problems differently than men. Unlike earlier studies, this study investigated the actual moral behavior of women in positions of power and leadership. Using the narrative method of inquiry, the author conducted in-depth interviews with 12 women who held positions of power and leadership in business organizations. The author oriented the in-depth interviews to gather information on the women's ethical frameworks and whether the frameworks gleaned from the interviews influenced their moral actions.

The findings from this research revealed that women in positions of power and leadership applied various forms of moral reasoning in their ethical practice and have a limited ability to articulate or to reflect upon how they arrived at their decisions. Additionally, the women in the study cited the fear of being disempowered as the greatest inhibitor to reflective thinking and moral creativity at work. This finding confirmed the hypothesis of the study. The key implications gleaned from the study suggest that businesspeople would benefit from educational training programs on ethics and morality within the workplace. Also, women in positions of power and leadership would benefit from exposure to the lessons learned in organizations that actively educate their executives in ethical decision-making and emphasize the public discussion of ethical dilemmas.

In a 2008 study conducted by E. Samier, the problem of passive evil in educational administration was examined through the lens of moral agency. One of the theories proposed by Samier to approach the problem was Bum's theory, which suggested:

> If one approaches the problem from a humanistic
> perspective and one that requires leadership, Bum's
> advocacy of "transforming" leadership, which
> is one of the theories which takes into account
> moral principle, sociocultural, political factors,
> psychological and intellectual wherewithal to bring
> about the change in values and resulting behavior,

could actually improve in moral terms, the lives of people in organizations.[101]

Moral leadership was described as an:

> Educative function embracing ethics and politics, grounded in personally held moral principle and "hard-nosed" pragmatist, achieved through a "symbiotic relationship" between leader and followers based in dissensus, that is, meaningful conflict necessary in the change process causing a transformation in social relations and political institutions. Above all, it is authentically morally purposeful, elevating both leader and followers "to more principled levels of judgment."[102]

I have often wondered why some employers assumed leaders come prepackaged with the skills necessary to lead with ethics and morality. I think employers make the assumption that a certain level of ethical competency has been obtained, but how these employers determine competency has never been clear to me. It is these individuals who often must make ethical decisions for their institutions.

In DeMethra Bradley's doctoral dissertation, "Outside First-Generation Inside-Second-Generation: Shedding Light on a Hidden Population in Higher Education," she coined the phrase "value capital." She described value capital as "being salient in how students navigate the college experience with peers and faculty, staff, and administrators. Value capital represents a fundamental set of understandings, a way to evaluate and make meaning of experiences."[103] I draw my value capital and *ethical capital* from my graduate school coursework on ethics, morality, and leadership as well as the family values I was raised with and practice every day. I am no longer naive in thinking other leaders draw their values from the same places that I draw mine.

Coping Strategies

In their book, *Leading with Authenticity in Times of Transition*, Kerry A. Bunker and Michael Wakefield argued that the bar has been raised for leaders since 9/11 and corporate scandals like Enron. Bunker wrote, "People want the strength and courage that characterized the stereotypical leader of the past; they also hold leaders to a high standard of character, humanness, and ability to empathize and care about others." As suggested by Bunker, leaders should focus on building trust with their employees, as opposed to the traditional one-sided approaches (such as micromanaging) used in the past; leaders can be strong, trusting, emphatic, and committed to change all at the same time.[104]

Bunker illustrates his point using the image of a wheel with the word trust at its center. Stemming from the center of the wheel are spokes that represent the 12 leader competencies that he believes leaders implement to deal with change and transition. Six of these spokes represent structural competencies, while the other six represent people-related competencies. Bunker's framework highlights how any of the 12 competencies "could be overdone, underdone, or held in a positive, dynamic balance: If a leader neglected or overplayed any one element, he strained the trust that would be needed to lead effectively during time of transition."[105]

Bunker's 12 competencies are as follows:

1. **Catalyzing change** is championing an initiative or significant change, consistently promoting the cause, and encouraging others to get on board.
2. **Coping with transition** is about recognizing and addressing the personal and emotional elements of change. It includes being in touch with your own emotions and reactions.
3. **Sense of urgency** involves taking action when necessary to keep things rolling. A leader who has a strong sense of urgency moves fast on issues and accelerates the pace of change for everyone.
4. **Realistic patience** requires knowing when and how to slow the pace to allow time and space for people to cope and adapt.
5. **Being tough** denotes the ability to make difficult decisions about issues and people with little hesitation or second-guessing.

6. **Being empathetic** involves taking others' perspectives into account when making decisions and taking action.
7. **Optimism** is the ability to see the positive potential of any challenge and to convey that optimism to others.
8. **Realism and openness** involve a willingness to be candid and clear about a situation and prospects for the future. It includes speaking the truth and admitting personal mistakes and foibles.
9. **Self-reliance** involves a willingness to take a lead role or even to do something yourself when necessary. A leader who is self-reliant has a great deal of confidence and is willing to step up and tackle most new challenges.
10. **Trusting others** means being comfortable with allowing others to do their part of a task or project. It includes being open to others for input and support.
11. **Capitalizing on strengths** entails knowing your strengths and attributes and confidently applying them to tackle new situations and circumstances.
12. **Going against the grain** involves a willingness to learn and try new things, to get out of your comfort zone, even when the process is difficult or painful.[106]

I have led several change initiatives in more than 35 years in leadership, and developing my leadership competencies has been a work in progress. Developing leadership competencies is a journey, not a destination. Many of the competencies shared by Bunker have worked for me in the past. Furthermore, his reference to 9/11 resonated with me. I recall exactly where I was when I learned our nation was under attack on September 11, 2001. I was on a leadership retreat, about to present a major change initiative with the other leaders in my division at my former university in North Carolina. That was in the days when cell phones were still a luxury, not a necessity. We all carried pagers back then, and they all started beeping and buzzing at the same time. In those days, our environment was so rigid and structured that not one of us visually or verbally acknowledged that a national disaster had just happened.

We went on with our business and ended our meeting at the planned time.

I was the only woman in a group of 25 men, and there was only one Black man among them. I remember thinking to myself, *Oh my God, what kind of place am I working in when airplanes are flying into the twin towers in New York City, one of our country's pride and jewels, and no one in the group publicly acknowledged what happened.* No one said, "You know what, folks, we've just had a national disaster. Let's take a moment and pause, pray, and check in with our families and employees to see how people are handling this situation." It was not even suggested. All of the division's leaders were in this meeting, and no one left.

After that happened, whatever respect I had for senior management was gone. I felt like leaving the meeting, but I knew my emotion surrounding the disaster would not go unnoticed, and I would be stereotyped as an overly emotional woman. An emotional response would not have been acceptable in that kind of working environment. *I have got to get the hell out of this job*, I thought. For a long time, my perception had been that my organization was dysfunctional, but their actions confirmed it for me that day. That experience helped to reiterate to me that I was not working in a very humanistic environment.

Fayneese Miller shares her experiences as the Dean of Education in one of the largest colleges at UVM in her essay titled, "Untangling the Ivory Vines: A Perspective on Women of Color in Higher Education." Miller opens with an analysis of the media's coverage of Michelle Obama and their fixation on her sense of fashion. She asks, "Has the media reaction to the first lady's preference for sleeveless dresses been influenced by the fact that Michelle Obama is a Black woman?" Miller interrogates the media's fixation on Michelle Obama's arms and uses it as a pretext for her discussion of women of color in higher education. She pointedly asks, "Do women of color face the same kind of judgment in the academy [higher education]?"[107]

Miller uses her experience at UVM to illustrate similarities between Mrs. Obama's experience and her own. The exploration of her experience as a woman of color change agent is significant, as she describes in detail how she negotiated her role as a senior administrator to navigate her way to overcoming the obstacles and challenges she encountered as a change agent. In sharing her story at UVM, Miller referenced Rossman's conceptual framework on emotional theory, which proposes, "The way a person reacts to another has much to do with how they relate past, present, and future events to their own goals and strivings."[108] Miller's story gives voice to a population of women of color who represent less than three percent of the senior administrators in higher education and who have even fewer representatives among nonacademic senior administrators.[109]

Stephen Brookfield, a leading scholar in continuing education, adult education, and diversity in the classroom, suggests that some leaders employ "deviant brownie point credits" when dealing with change. They do what they need to as a leader so that they do not get marginalized by leading one type of change. This frees them up to be taken seriously when they pursue other initiatives. He also argues that leaders are often not given training on how to navigate the political landscape in the academy. Therefore, mentoring could be helpful.[110]

Beverly A. Cropper and Philomena Harrison provide yet another lens through which to analyze Black women's experiences in the paper, "Real or Imagined—Black Women's Experiences in the Academy." The authors borrow from the autobiographical and theoretical writings of Black women such as Patricia Hill Collins, bell hooks, Andre Lorde, and Toni Morrison because they believe Black feminist theory has been useful and meaningful due to its ability to accommodate differences and commonalities between Black women, which other feminist discourses and single-issue discourses have failed to do.[111] Additionally, the concept of sharing common experiences—the engagement in self-conscious struggle—has been a necessary process through which Black women have defined for themselves who they are and how they wish to be engaged in resisting and surviving discrimination and oppression. The interdependence between thought and action is an important factor within Black feminist thought and is a theme that permeates these authors' work.

In another study conducted by Sidney H. Barksdale in 2007, she demonstrates how many of the obstacles and barriers for Black women described by earlier scholars still exist. Barksdale conducted a study on the coping strategies of Black women working at a PWI. The phrase "othermothering" described the coping strategy results that came out of her study. The concept of transformational womanism and othermothering frameworks are not new and were applied to all of the women's stories in Barksdale's study. As quoted in Barksdale, the term "womanism" was coined by Alice Walker, who defined womanism as a "populist and poetic synonyms for Black feminist and Black feminism."[112]

Many of the women in Barksdale's study attributed their success in navigating the obstacles and barriers in the workplace to the support they gained from the relationships formed with other women of color.[113] The same networks were invaluable in helping these women adjust to their new environment in other areas, such as childcare, housing, healthcare referrals, and grooming. While this was not a formal organization recognized by the institution, it appeared to be a good resource for the women in the study. I believe the concept of "othermothering" has some value for women like me working in PWIs; however, it is not for everyone. I recall discussing this concept with another Black woman who found it offensive and did not want to be lumped into this type of category simply because she was a Black woman.

Experience has taught me that the more responsibility I assume, the more vulnerable I am. When the shit hits the fan, the people in my confidence circle are the ones who will be there to support me. I believe it is critical for Black women in leadership roles to surround themselves with people who will lend encouragement and consultation—and *pray*, not *prey* on them—when that is all that can be done with a situation. Putting our faith in our belief system and those we serve because we know we have demonstrated what it is to be an ethical leader every day has sustained the courageous Black women leading in PWIs, but at what cost? I think institutions have made some gains in their recruitment efforts of Black women in PWIs, but I wonder how many of those hires have led to longevity in those institutions. Have those women's experiences been similar to my own? If they were successful in sustaining their leadership, how did they do it? Would they have similar experiences to share? My experiences being reflected and validated in the literature seems to suggest that this is a universal theme among Black women leading in PWIs.

Some scholars have suggested mentoring programs as a vehicle for retention. Judith A. Aiken and Wanda Heading-Grant's study, "Cross Culture Mentoring Relationships," focused on faculty of color in the academy (higher education). According to the study's authors, "Cross-race mentoring raises special issues that are absent in the typical white male-to-male relationships, especially when the mentoring relationship is between white male mentors and female mentees of color."[114] Furthermore, Chao and colleagues (1992) argued that the basic distinction between formal and informal mentorship is the formation of the mentor/mentee relationship. The formal mentoring relationship is typically supported by institutions and provides opportunities for all faculty and underrepresented populations,[115] whereas an informal mentorship has been defined as a "spontaneous relationship without external involvement from the organization." As Redmond asserted in the same study, "Informal mentoring is perceived as less likely to happen with faculty of color, especially in PWIs."[116]

While I believe mentoring has its place, my experience has taught me that depending on one's career level a sponsorship would be warranted. My observation has been that men often have more access to these types of opportunities than women.

Heading-Grant and Aiken suggested:

> The multicultural realities in higher education
> call for mentors who can effectively address the
> challenges that can come with diversity. Cross-
> racial mentoring is a fact of life for most junior
> faculty of color, given the current racial makeup

of higher education. In order to engage effectively in diversified mentoring, it would be important to examine the effect of an institutionally designed, ongoing professional development process focused on cultural competence.[117]

The authors further presented an emerging theme of cross-racial mentoring. Before you can help someone else, you need to know your own heritage.[118] The authors suggested networking internally and externally of the organization as a resource for mentees beyond the mentoring relationship. Additionally, the authors suggested institutions should encourage access to these kinds of resources in the future.

Kijana Crawford and Danielle Smith conducted a research study on the mentoring of Black women in PWIs. The study investigated the importance of mentoring in Black women's selection of higher education as a career choice and in their development as professionals in that career. The research clarified how mentoring affected the career choices of Black women who became administrators in higher education and how their socio-cultural and gender experiences defined their career choices and development. This study defined mentoring as:

> The sharing of power, information, and self. An
> effective mentor can advance the acceptance
> of a talented individual into an inner circle.
> The task of the mentor is to afford the protégé
> with opportunities to learn and practice and to
> reward him or her so that acquired knowledge,
> performance, and motivation increase.[119]

The significant findings from this study were:

1. Mentoring in the traditional definition affected the career choices and development of the women in the study because none of them experienced a process by which an individual of superior rank, special achievements, or prestige instructed, counseled, guided, or facilitated their intellectual or career development.

2. None of the women were socialized by a senior member to the rules and culture of the academy. The women in the study did not receive the benefits of being in a situation where their leadership ability was cultivated. They had been educated and trained but not nurtured. Most of the women's career choices and development had been circumstantial and unplanned. The women were frustrated and felt isolated because they were not noticed or observed by a mentor to determine whether future contributions would be viable or if special attributes were present.

3. It was noted that a senior mentor usually has access to an inner circle of institutional gatekeepers, as well as in-depth knowledge about the academy. The incremental hierarchical mentoring that would allow the mentor an opportunity to formulate and judge the mentee's ability to handle difficult dilemmas had not been afforded these female administrators.

4. None of these women had been given the opportunity to learn the ropes before accepting challenging work or assignments that would demonstrate their competence. Nor had they been given the responsibilities of standards related to professional behavior and performance, such as establishing a relationship, ascertaining the predictability of the working relationship, or maintaining a major influence in the selection and development of their career choice. The participants believed that if they had the benefit of a mentor, they would have had greater job satisfaction.

5. As cited in Crawford and Smith, research by Reich in 1985 indicates that female protégés specifically reported elevated self-confidence, enhanced opportunities for creativity, and opportunities for increased development of their skills.

6. As cited in Crawford and Smith, research by Ilgen and Youtz in 1986 also noted that female employees without mentors were less effective on the job. Mentoring has shown promise as an appropriate intervention for advancing the careers of the mentee. People with mentors have reported greater productivity and career development. They have also exhibited greater productivity as leaders

in professional associations, received more competitive grants, and published more articles in their fields.

7. The women as a group were dissatisfied with their careers. When asked what they were aspiring to, the women seemed to be looking for their next jobs as opposed to developing and honing their skills.[120]

Throughout these chapters, I have shared my experience of not having formal mentors to help guide my professional development. The informal mentoring that I gained from the SHEROs in my personal life was not sufficient enough to help me navigate my career. My professional career was treading on a path that was unknown to them. Even though I did not have formal mentors, I learned through reading self-help books how to reach out to other people for help. Even though I did not have role models like me to advise me, I did reach out to anyone who had the skills I desired to have to help me develop as a leader. It is important to note that I had to go outside of my profession to find people who were willing to advise me. I did not discriminate; I reached out to all races, genders, and ages. If a person had something they could teach me, I was a sponge, ready to absorb the knowledge. My self-selection of informal mentors, some younger than me, were White men and women in different professions who offered a diverse wealth of experience and knowledge for me to draw upon.

Networking is another valuable coping strategy for Black women leaders. I was reminded about this when I attended an open forum at UVM during HOMEcoming in 2011. Several of the alumni from 1980 through 2010 had been asked to share their experiences on a panel as UVM undergraduate students of color. It was a pretty diverse panel. I recall two members of the panel, one Black man from the class of 1980 and one Hispanic woman from the class of 1981, suggesting to students that they should not look at color when forging networking opportunities because they believed "not seeing color" is what helped them get through their four years at UVM and later in their professional careers.

Leslye Renee Kornegay, EdD

The Black male panelist talked about spending his spare time at UVM taking golf lessons through the physical education department and how he had just come from golfing in Istanbul.

The Hispanic woman on the panel shared that she is a first-generation Mexican American who went into computer science, a nontraditional field for women, especially women of color. She explained that her dad was her biggest advocate, encouraging her to excel because she was just as good as the men she was in school with at the time.

On the other hand, a Black woman on the panel who had graduated in 2010 painted a very different picture of the environment. All she had seen was her differences at the institution, and it was not a pleasant experience for her. I thought it was interesting how different each of those UVM alumni's experiences were. I was raised to see the person first versus the color of their skin. It has become second nature to me. However, it has not prevented others from judging me based on my color.

Letter to Black Women in Higher Education

I am waiting for them to stop talking about the Other, to stop even describing how important it is to be able to speak about difference...Often their speech about the Other is a mask, an oppressive talk hiding gaps, absences, that space where our words would be if we were speaking. Often this speech about the Other annihilates, erases: No need to hear your voice when we can talk about you better than you can speak about yourself. Only tell me about your pain. I want to know your story. And then I will tell it back to you in a new way. Tell it back to you in such a way that it has become mine, my own. Re-writing you, I write myself anew. I am still author, authority, I am still the colonizer, the speaking subject, and you are now at the centre of my talk, Stop.[121]
—bell hooks

Dear Black Women in Leadership,

If you are a Black woman leader working in a PWI, chances are what I am about to share with you will not be a surprise.

The 2010 Bureau of Labor Statistics annual household data averages for management/professional occupations present a pretty optimistic perception of Black women's representation in the private sector. Interestingly, White women have become the new gatekeepers (the establishment that dictates the established norms) at 41.5 percent, White males coming in second at 38.5 percent, followed by Black women at 33.8 percent.[122]

When it comes to higher education, the statistics for Black women serving in executive roles are significantly reduced. The American Council on Education (ACE) reported that the percentage of women presidents in the ACE increased from 10 percent in 1986 to 23 percent in 2006. The increase for women presidents of color was smaller, with an increase from 3 percent in 1986 to 14 percent in 2006. When disaggregated by race/ethnicity, of that 14 percent in 2006, 6.6 percent of the women presidents were Hispanic, 1.0 percent were Asian-American, 1.5 percent were Indigenous American, 8.1 percent were Black, and 8.1 percent were White. William B. Harvey and Eugene L. Anderson reported that in 2004, out of 200 women executives of public four-year institutions, eighteen (9 percent) were Black, eight (4 percent) were Hispanic, two (1 percent) were Indigenous American, and one (0.5 percent) was Asian American. Meanwhile, 171 (85.5 percent) were White.[123]

You might be wondering why these statistics are significant. Why should it matter to you? As cited in Patricia Hill Collins, the exclusion of Black women's ideas from mainstream academic discourse and the curious placement of Black women intellectuals in both feminist and Black social and political thought have meant that Black women intellectuals have remained outsiders within all three communities.[124]

Additionally, Hill Collins wrote,

> The assumptions on which full group membership
> are based—whiteness for feminist thought, maleness
> for Black social and political thought, and the
> combination for mainstream scholarship—all negate
> a Black female reality.[125]

Black women, "prevented from becoming full insiders in any of these areas of inquiry, remain outsiders within, individuals whose marginality provides a distinctive angle of vision on the theories put forth by such intellectual communities."[126] I believe this is significant because it overwhelmingly shows that Black women in executive leadership roles in higher education have only yielded a slight increase over the past 20 years. White women and White men continue to be the majority groups in executive leadership positions within higher education administration.[127] This would account for the fact that most of the research in the area of women in leadership has been dominated by White women and seen through the lens of White women and White men.

Women in positions of power and leadership would benefit from exposure to the lessons learned in organizations that actively educate their more senior executives in ethical decision making and emphasize the public discussion of ethical dilemmas. Their employers offered no ethical training opportunities yet they were expected to make ethical decisions in the workplace. The ethical training that I have received has been a result of my graduate and doctoral studies, which has prepared me well. I often draw from that knowledge to work through ethical decisions and dilemmas in my workplace.

I believe it is essential for the dominant group to understand their own history before they can understand our culture. This is especially true working in PWIs. Developing this skill comes with being culturally and emotionally competent and should be embraced by all higher education senior executives. I encourage you to investigate an organization's climate before applying for employment. If you are working in a PWI, develop support networks "confidence circles" and alliances that can help you navigate challenges when they occur.

Like many of you, I have endured racism, sexism, genderism, and classism in the workplace, and I have emerged as a stronger leader in spite of it. I have drawn my strength from my faith, family/HOME, informal mentors, and confidence circles, continuing my education and learning how to take care of my health.

The concept of "shifting" to sustain your role in the academy is not new to some of you. It's a carryover from slavery and Jim Crow. Our coping strategies are many:

Speaking one way in the office, another way to your
friends and family; working overtime when you
are exhausted to prove you are not lazy; learning
how to ignore a comment you believe is racist or to
address it in such a way that the person who said it
does not label you threatening or aggressive; over-
preparing for a course to prove that you are just as
capable as your peers who have more social capital
than you do; keeping a positive attitude about
yourself regardless what society projects you to be;
or finding the need to fight back.[128]

Transforming ourselves to sustain our roles is nothing new.
While I suggest it's a common experience that we share, I am
aware that some of you might be unwilling to embrace some
of the lessons learned in this letter. I offer them as examples of
some of my own experiences working in PWIs as well as what
the literature has to offer on our experiences.

What has been new for me in my journey that I want to
share with you has been finding my womanist voice along the
way. As a leader, I have been able to sustain my leadership by
learning how to construct a style that embraces who I am as a
Black woman. In doing so, I have found my voice as a leader,
and I have learned to name racist and sexist acts of oppression
in my personal and professional life.

The benefits of having a career and/or life mentor are
critical for Black women in leadership. If you do not have
someone mentoring you who looks like you in your profession,
I advise you to reach out to people inside and outside of your
profession or environment who are in roles you aspire to be.
Look outside of your race and gender. If someone in a senior
executive role is willing to sponsor or mentor you, by all means
give it some serious consideration. What do you have to lose?
Consider having more than one mentor because depending on
the nature of the job or what you are aspiring to become, you
might need multiple mentors.

Asking for help is hard; it's a fear I had to get over. If you
have a fear of asking for help, I suggest exploring with yourself
where that fear stems from and working to overcome it. You

can use my experiences in my narratives as a starting point. Additionally, if you are in a position where you can mentor up-and-coming women like yourself, by all means, find the time to do it. Who else will do it if you do not? Many of you have already answered to the responsibility of uplifting others as described earlier; it's what has been expected when we are the first and only ones in our families and communities to obtain a degree or achieve a certain status. Black women have historically embraced the responsibility to uplift people who are coming up behind them by mentoring and providing resources.

I hope you choose to share your experiences working in PWIs by contributing to the scholarship on Black women. Only then can we become a more visible population in the literature. I believe Scholarly Personal Narrative (SPN) writing for leaders and students of color in higher education can be a useful tool in helping women like us develop meaning-making of our experiences in PWIs. SPN is a great method for sharing our stories because the writer is not bound to any set order (i.e. placing personal history into any chronological order), and the personal narrative and themes are grounded in scholarly research. Robert Nash, the creator of SPN writing, described the origin of the word "narrative" as the Greek word *narro*, which means *to survive*.[129] Relating the word narrative to survive resonated with me because Black women have been surviving since the days of slavery. Throughout history, Black women have demonstrated that we know how to lead with emotional intelligence.[130] The rich resources that could be provided to aspiring leaders through the lessons learned from their life experiences would be critical for their leadership development. I think James Baldwin, one of the most well-known Black writers of the 20th century, said it eloquently in *Writing to Change the World:*

> You write in order to change the world, knowing perfectly well that you probably can't, but also knowing that literature is indispensable to the world. ... The world changes according to the way people see it, and if you alter, even by a millimeter, the way ... people look at reality, then you can change it.[131]

I believe SPN writing would also benefit formal mentoring and sponsoring programs where the mentees can share their experiences with their mentors. This would offer another vehicle for mentors/sponsors to provide support to their mentees. SPN writing reaches the masses who do not aspire to be researchers but who strive for meaning-making in their daily lives—yes, even women like me who are practitioners leading in PWIs. Every SPN is unique to the writer. There are as many SPN research designs as there are writers. What this means to you as a Black woman is that SPN is an opportunity for you to write in your *strongest* voice. I hope you find some of the tips I have put together in this letter helpful as you navigate the waters in your workplace. I will continue on my journey, and I hope you will continue on with yours.

Best wishes,

Leslye

Chapter Five: Kornegay Journey to Doctor of Education

Finding my voice and learning how to advocate for myself has evolved over time. I did not fully realize my intellectual identity until I entered UVM's Educational and Leadership Studies program. Having lived more than 60 years of life as a Black woman with Native American and Irish heritage, I had carried around my share of baggage. Melba Joyce Boyd, a professor at Wayne State University, shared her experiences growing up in the South post-1960 in "Disappearing Acts: Black Face and the Tyranny of Intellectual Imperialism."[132]

> This memory re-emerges from time to time, especially when I must engage unsubstantiated critiques of my work or engage in defense of assistant professors and graduate students for whom collegial consideration stings as deeply as my first grade teacher's tongue lashing for helping a struggling classmate sound out a word. I came to understand that I am one of those "uppity Negroes" who doesn't know her place. But since I come from a long line of "uppity Negroes," for me it was a badge of courage, which was sorely needed when I became an adult and entered graduate school, immediately after receiving my bachelor's degree.[133]

I have learned it is not how much baggage you carry around in this life that matters, but rather it is what you have done with that baggage that counts. I chose not to accept the victim role when faced with daily microaggressions, such as discrimination and hostile work environments. If you can channel the load you carry into something positive instead of letting it dictate your successes, you can live your best life. When I finally found my voice, I learned that I am a womanist, and I choose to tell my story through the lenses of social justice and womanism.

In 2008, I made the decision to pursue a doctorate in Educational Leadership and Policy Studies (EDLP) at UVM. That program enabled me to focus my research in an area that had been near and dear to my heart: Black women in higher education senior administration. Finally, I would be able to answer some of the challenging questions I had identified very early in my career, including: Why are there so few women like me in higher education executive leadership positions? How had the Black women who had made it to the executive role done it? Who taught them how to lead? How did they sustain their leadership? What challenges, barriers, and obstacles had they encountered working in PWIs? And how had they overcome those challenges? Was my story the exception? Or was it the norm?

My Research Passion

When I began my study at EDLP, I found it was a natural fit for me and was a continuation of the journey I began in 1997. The program was unlike anything I had previously been exposed to. It encouraged members in my cohort to ask questions that challenged the status quo. I began to see infinite possibilities, and I realized that my perception and outlook on life had been limited by the worldview of the dominant group in our society: White men.

I was exposed to a full breadth and depth of theorists, and I discovered that people actually studied what I had been doing the past 30-plus years, only through the lens of the dominant group. I realized that the application processes researchers wrote about were things I had practiced in my leadership roles. What I did not find in the literature were women with unique backgrounds like me that could compare to my leadership experiences as a Black woman executive in the academy. I wanted to conduct research to add to the growing body of scholarship.

The EDLP program introduced me to the major theorists, ideologies, and concepts in my area of study. The program helped me to identify the key research that had been conducted in higher education. I was drawn to theorists who contributed to the body of work in Black Feminism, Womanism, Leadership, Social Theory, Social Justice, Ethical Theory, and Social Reproduction. During that time in my educational journey, I realized this kind of research had my name written all over it, which confirmed my desire to be an instrument of change for Black women in higher education. I recall seeing very little research conducted on Black women in executive leadership in higher education. The literature that did exist was limited to the presidency level.

Additionally, during the EDLP program, when reading the book *Character of Leadership,* it occurred to me that Machiavelli's leadership method, despite being written centuries ago, was well at work in the modern-day leadership held by the dominant groups—White men and White women.[134]

I remember thinking about how Machiavelli's work was banished during his lifetime, yet modern-day elements of leadership draw from Machiavelli's methods, such as virtu, hermeneutic of suspicion, sense of smell, political savvy, reality vs. ideology, and the sense of touch.[135] I found myself wondering, Why does history continue to repeat itself? Why do some leaders fail while others succeed? Because Machiavelli's work focused on the men in leadership roles during his day, if his research had included women, would the lessons learned be the same? Because society was basically patriarchal during Machiavelli's time (1469-1527), were the failures attributed only to the dominant group (White male leaders) because women were not observed as leaders? Or could Machiavelli's principles have been applied to all leaders regardless of gender, race, or ethnicity?

Additionally, I wondered how ethical leadership and the other leadership styles would have been factored into the successes and/or failures of those types of leaders if they had been included in Machiavelli's work. I have often wondered whether Machiavelli was acting in a mentor role when he advised the Prince Lorenzo de Medici in around the year 1513. Much of my research has been focused on trying to understand these kinds of questions as they relate to Black women in leadership.

I Still DREAM That ONE DAY

My cohort experience was much like other experiences in life where I had adjusted—yes, *shifted*—to fit into the group. Once again, I was the only person of color. I recall feeling a little apprehensive and questioning whether this was really my calling. Once the coursework began in earnest, I realized that the course content addressed controversial real-world issues, not viewing them through rose-colored lenses, and that the professors were really social change agents trying to raise social consciousness among all of us. That's when I knew I had made the right decision to join the EDLP program. The program allowed for a safe space where I could express myself—most of the time, at least. While many of my experiences in the program were positive, sometimes I felt like an outsider in my cohort. Being the only person of color, I found myself drawing upon my adapting skills to bridge two worlds.

Another point of difference was the fact that most of my peers came into the course with social capital that I did not have, especially from my K-12 educational experience. A number of scholars talk about social capital and upward mobility.

For example, the book *Ain't No Makin' It* by Jay MacLeod portrays the structural inequality that perpetuates poverty in a captivating way. Through a comparative analysis of the aspirations and attainments of two separate groups, one of which buys into the achievement ideology, while the other outright rejects it, the reader is able to see barriers created even when individuals bought into the idea of the "American Dream."

According to MacLeod, "By embodying class interests and ideologies, schools reward the cultural capital of the dominant classes and systematically devalue that of the lower classes."[136] If you are not a part of the dominant group, your cultural capital is not recognized as an asset. According to MacLeod:

Bourdieu's theory maintains that the cultural capital of the lower-classes—their manners, norms, dress, style of interaction, and linguistic facility—is devalued by the school, while the cultural capital of the upper classes is rewarded.[137]

S. Dumais suggested:

To acquire cultural capital, a student must have the ability to receive and internalize it. Although schools require that students have this ability, they do not provide it for them; rather, the acquisition of cultural capital is passed down by the family, which, in turn, is largely dependent on social class.[138]

According to Bourdieu (1973, as cited in Dumais, 2002):

.... the school system rewards students who have cultural capital; the ultimate reward is in the form of educational credentials (institutionalized cultural capital), but along the way, students with higher cultural capital receive better grades and more attention and feedback.[139]

Additionally, a link has been shown to the lack of cultural capital and growing up in low-income neighborhoods. Socio-economic status has been shown to impact the amount of cultural participation at a greater rate than gender. According to Dumais:

Within the SES [social economic status] groups, however, the difference between boys' and girls' art museum attendance was 0 percentage points for low-SES and 8 percentage points for high-SES students. Even going to the public library, the most popular activity for all students, was far less likely to occur for low-SES students than for high-SES students.[140]

Due to the structural inequalities existent in Clarendon Heights and the low socioeconomic status of the study participants, they did not have access to cultural participation activities.

Education and Social Capital

Of the two groups being observed, the Brothers bought into the achievement ideology and viewed America as the land of opportunity.[141] According to MacLeod:

> These viewpoints are consistent with the dominant ideology in America; barriers to success are seen as personal rather than social. By attributing failure to personal inadequacy, the Brothers exonerate the opportunity structure. Indeed, it is amazing how they affirm the openness of American society.[142]

The Brothers were dedicated to their academics and bought into the assertion that education levels the playing field. MacLeod went on to write, "As the achievement ideology propagated in school implies, education is viewed as the remedy for the problem of social inequality; schooling makes the race for prestigious jobs and wealth an even one."[143] The Hallway Hangers (the name of the other group in the study) did not believe in the open structure and did not buy into the achievement ideology. According to MacLeod, "The ideology is not as emotionally painful for the Brothers to accept because past racial discrimination can help account for their families' poverty, whereas the Hallway Hangers, if the ideology stands, are afforded no explanation outside of laziness and stupidity for their parents' failures."[144]

As I unpack the findings from the Brothers and Hallway Hangers, it is clear my experiences are more like the Brothers than the Hallway Hangers. Like the extended family of the Brothers, habits and cultural capital directly affected my social circumstances.[145] I am the only one of my mother's children to graduate from college. And while we never lived in a low-income housing complex like Clarendon Heights (in Boston, which MacLeod visited and described in his work), we did live in the rural South during some of my childhood where racism and segregation were prominent. I believe that I was not exposed to racism until I was a young adult in the workplace. I was always in pursuit of my degree, but I never applied myself to completing the journey until I ran into the cement ceiling as a woman of color in a PWI. Like the Brothers, I believed if I obtained an advanced degree, I would improve my human capital and upward mobility and it would happen automatically. Like the Brothers, I quickly realized this is not how it happens for women and people of color in America. The Hallway Hangers' perception that people of color automatically receive promotions and upward mobility due to affirmative action was not my experience. To achieve career development, like the members who were successful, relocating helped me obtain upward mobility. Subsequently, I hit the proverbial cement ceiling in my profession being a Black woman and, in response, uprooted myself from my family and friends and relocated to Vermont to follow my calling in leadership. Cultural and social capital has become ever present in my everyday life as I navigate the academy in my two roles as both student and executive.

During MacLeod's second visit to Clarendon Heights in 1991, he illustrated the impact of race in the equation of success, saying, "Of the Hallway Hangers, the two black members—Boo-Boo and Chris—are in the most desperate straits. And of the Brothers, the sole white member—Mike—has been far and away the most successful on the job market."[146] Through interviews at mid-life, MacLeod found similar results and McClelland and Karen stated:

> The predominance of Hallway Hangers at the bottom is not surprising, but their presence near the top is. The four most successful among the group—the only ones to have attained the key components of their definition of success—include two Hangers and two Brothers; three were white and only one was black. The two who fail completely out of the race—Boo-Boo and Chris—were the black members of the Hallway Hangers.[147]

Ain't No Makin' It exposed the struggles of race and class as they intersect for members of the Hangers and the Brothers. MacLeod noted:

Racism is a sickness that rots American society, but those who see it simply as a matter of individual pathology overlook the social conditions that contribute to its outbreak and spread. We can blame the Hallway Hangers, but we also must blame the economic and social conditions of lower-class life under competitive capitalism.[148]

According to MacLeod, "Once we push beneath the surface texts of individual lives, we discover the hard contours of structural inequality. Our society is structured to create poverty and extreme economic inequality."[149]

I have seen stories like that of the Hallway Hangers and the Brothers play out in my student and executive experience, and I feel that *Ain't No Makin' It* provides an accurate portrayal of the structural barriers in place that perpetuate the inequitable class system. Having lived in Green Acres as a child, then going to lead and work with the most marginalized population on my university campus, as well as hearing my family's and friends' stories, it is evident that social reproduction is alive and well and being played out through our schools, and also our families, communities, agencies, and institutional systems.

Through the stories of the Hallway Hangers and the Brothers of Clarendon Heights, we are provided only a glimpse into their lives growing up in an impoverished community. *Ain't No Makin' It* provided me another window to understand systematic oppression around race and class. The Hallway Hangers and Brothers made me realize how much more I needed to learn about the class divides in our society and how social classes are maintained in part through our education system. As a doctoral student and executive leader, I was a product of this dysfunctional system. I have struggled my entire adult life to overcome some of the scars I have been afflicted with from our flawed K-12 educational system. While I carried these scars into my higher education academic experience, I have not let them define my success as a student. I have had to work harder than other people, but I have proven that I have just as much right to be here as my peers who arrived with more social capital than me.

My doctoral program peers were sociable, but only a few of them actually forged a strong connection with me during my experience that I believe will be lifelong. I have heard former cohort members share stories of the bonding and support that they gave each other to ensure that they all were successful in completing the program. I am not sure what happened with my cohort, but most of us went our separate ways once we completed the core courses with the exception of my writing partner, Christina Olstad.

Regardless, I excelled in the program. However, one core course toward the end of the required course load made me question whether I belonged in the program. Throughout my doctoral experience, I was able to bridge my doctoral work with my experiences on the job. In that particular course, I focused my project on a work-related change initiative. I shared milestones with my professor throughout the program. All of the feedback was positive. These professors (the chair of the doctoral program and the instructor for the course that I was in) were seasoned and very laid back in their approach. My final grade for the class was an A, but my professor had commented that unless I started to write in a more "scholarly" style, they did not know if I would make it in the program. This really hurt me, like Windy Paz-Amor shared in her SPN: "If you really want to hurt me, talk badly about my language. Ethnic identity is twin skin to linguistic identity. I am my language."[150] That professor provided no additional insight nor resources, just that very cutting statement about my ability to succeed in the doctoral program.

Fast forward two years later. I was taking an SPN class with Robert Nash and having the following conversation with my classmate:

> **Cindy:** I was trying to figure out how or where
> I have seen you before, and now I remember.
> Professor Colby raved about you in our class; he
> used your work as a model for all of us to do our
> project.
> **Leslye:** Really? Do you recall which course?

Cindy: Yes it was this (X) core course. He said your paper was an example of what all of us should strive for in order to be successful in his course.

Leslye: I am surprised. Can I share something with you confidentially?
Cindy: Yes, of course.
Leslye: I am really surprised he is using my work as a model for his classes, given that he criticized my writing and told me he was concerned about my writing style and whether I would be successful at the dissertation writing stage because it was too "common" and not "scholarly" enough.

That conversation left me feeling vindicated. Regardless of how my professor had labeled my work and abilities, I persevered only to be absolved two years later after learning that he was holding my work as a model project. If I had let him define what I was capable of at that time, I would have given up on my educational journey.

My UVM experience reminded me of another time when I was at the State University in North Carolina, asking myself, "what now?" after completing my master's degree. I called the college and spoke to someone about applying to the PhD program. She seemed very pleasant over the phone and suggested that I set up a time to stop by. I made the appointment and went to meet with her. She was an elderly White woman and not very friendly in person. She never asked me about my experience nor even to see a transcript, yet she proceeded to tell me that I would have a hard time getting into the program. She told me that before she would look at my application, I would need to take a doctoral-level course and prove to her that I could do that level of work. That was nothing like the positive response I had gotten from her over the phone—*before* she saw me in person. She made it very clear to me that would be the only way I would even be considered. If that had been normal protocol, surely she would have told me that over the phone. It felt like racism at its finest, and I allowed that experience to define my pursuit of a doctoral degree for a long time.

After completing my doctoral program's core course work successfully, I immediately formed my dissertation committee and began to frame my dissertation proposal. Originally, I wanted to do a qualitative study. I struggled for a while trying to fit a research design with what I wanted to do. I wrote a number of drafts, but really could not connect to what I was saying I wanted to do. I had been told repeatedly to focus my research on something that I am passionate about. If I didn't, I would run the risk of being All But Dissertation, or ABD. Because I had formed my first committee based on my professional ties with the university community, I disbanded the committee.

I had done an SPN independent study with Robert Nash, and we had developed a very strong student-professor relationship. I sought him out, discussed my research interest, and asked if he thought I could do an SPN dissertation. Like so many other SPN converts before me, we met at the infamous Chefs Corner for breakfast and two hours after we began talking, Robert confirmed for me that I could do an SPN dissertation on my topic and also that he would love to be on my committee. I cannot describe what this meant to me. Robert truly cared about his students; he wanted to see all of them be successful. He always made time to meet with me and to respond to my emails. I honestly do not know how he managed it because he did this for an entire community of students at all levels at the institution.

Having the approval to use the SPN methodology to conduct my research made all of the difference for me. I enlisted those faculty who had supported me throughout my journey along with Robert and the vice president of DEI to lead my dissertation committee. To ensure that I had a thorough understanding of SPN writing, I enrolled in Robert's SPN writing class. This was perhaps the single most validating experience I have ever had in higher education, and I felt that it should have been the model for other courses at the institution. On the very first day of his class, I felt like I was HOME. Students greeted each other with hugs and acknowledgments, which was totally different than what I was used to. Robert and DeMethra Bradley, who co-taught the class, did not lecture at us during the three-hour weekly course; they engaged us and created a community of respect that encouraged sharing.

Taking the SPN class and learning about this style of writing happened at the perfect time for me. Instead of dreading having to write something for class, I literally could not wait to write because I knew I had something valuable to share and my voice would be respected. Like my SPN instructors, I believe people who find and embrace SPN do not like to be limited. SPN frees the writer to be creative and let their writing inform the scholarship, not the other way around. I already knew I had a story to tell, but Robert helped me to find my scholarly voice through SPN.

My struggles as a sponsorless, mentorless normative Black executive, having experienced a 30-plus year journey into leadership, propelled me into a mission to conduct research on Black women like me and to bottle that knowledge up into a leadership model that truly reflected all of my experiences and lessons learned as a leader. My inspirations were fueled even more when the first Black man was elected to the Presidency of the United States. During my childhood years, it seemed our nation was always in tears. I vaguely recall the deaths of Martin Luther King Jr., John F. Kennedy, and Robert Kennedy. Since that time, society has come a long way toward realizing Dr. King's dream, but we still have more work to do.

On November 4, 2008, in what has become known as the "Grant Park Speech," President Obama delivered his now-famous victory speech, which was televised around the world. He opened the speech with the following statement:

> If there is anyone out there who still doubts that
> America is a place where all things are possible,
> who still wonder if the dream of our founders is
> alive in our time, who still question the power of
> our democracy, tonight is your answer.[151]

Although I am grateful that I have lived to see a Black man elected as the President of the United States, I cannot fully buy into the ideology that anybody can "make it" in America. It took 200 years for America to elect its first Black president, and we have yet to elect a woman into the President's office.

President Obama was born with social/cultural capital that the average Black person still does not hold. Being raised by his White mother and White grandparents in a predominately White environment cannot be compared to the average Black child's experience. Like President Obama's mother and grandparents, my parents exposed me to different cultures when I was young. However, unlike President Obama, having this social, cultural, and linguistic capital did not allow me to graduate from an Ivy League school at the top of my class.

While we have come a long way, we still have a lot of work to do in the area of equality and social justice. I think President Obama's acceptance speech, in part, espouses colonialism as a positive force in the rhetoric. How could he fondly embrace the founding fathers' practices when President Jefferson had children by his slave mistress while he was President? Or while our founding fathers continued using slaves as the primary source of labor in the masters' house. President Obama was supposed to be an agent of change, yet how can you tear down the masters' house using the masters' tools? The great poet Audre Lorde captured my thoughts eloquently in her famous quote:

> For the master's tools will never dismantle the master's house. They may allow us temporarily to beat him at his own game, but they will never enable us to bring about genuine change. And this fact is only threatening to those women who still define the master's house as their only source of support.[152]

President Obama's election was a momentous historical event that gave me a feeling of pride for all Black Americans. I felt pure excitement and joy, and I knew life would never be the same for all Americans. As I reflect back on that time, I believe I came away with the same renewed conviction that I can do anything I want to because the first Black President had become a reality in my lifetime. Since President Obama's tenure in the White House, researchers like Wanda V. Parham-Payne have begun to wonder if the success of his campaign will pave the way for women of color to one day secure the nomination of a major political party and subsequently be elected to the United States Presidency.[153]

When we gained our first Black President, we also gained our first Black First Lady. I believe Michelle Obama was just as charismatic as her husband. Charisma is a leadership trait that is a valuable tool if you are blessed enough to be born with it, and a number of other Presidents have been described as having this trait, including John F. Kennedy and Bill Clinton. Michelle Obama has role modeled a positive image of what a Black woman can be in our society. Even though she did not hold an official office, I submit that she, in her own way, was a leader for Black women to aspire to be in her roles as wife, mother, and First Lady of the United States.

I was once interviewed by Stuart Ledbetter, a journalist with the local Vermont television news, who was curious about my thoughts on the election. I described the excitement in the air. At the time, Black people were really energized and optimistic about the implications of having someone they could identify with in the White House.[154] There was a real sense of hope for a better future for everyone, and I thought that, if something like this could happen then surely my research could serve as a resource for other Black women aspiring to ascend into executive roles within institutions of higher learning.

I no longer ask myself if my research goals have value. I know they do, and it is important to understand at a societal level why Black women continue to be underrepresented in the senior executive echelons in our institutions of higher learning. Our stories need to be heard on the global level. I hope that the lessons learned can serve as a resource for anyone who wants to understand the challenges and dilemmas that Black women have to navigate on a daily basis. A societal change is long overdue.

Leslye Renee Kornegay, EdD

Letter to Self

Dear Leslye,

You have lived through multiple historic changes in American society and witnessed how they have impacted Black women. You have also heard your elders' stories around the oppressive conditions experienced by Black women before you were born. You were able to witness societal transitions into a reality in which women have been able to embrace the freedom of choice, to decide what they will do with their lives on their own terms.

All of the women on the maternal side of your family are strong and independent, and they have all worked outside of the HOME while being the primary caretakers. The words of your mother have echoed throughout your childhood and adult years. *"You are not defined by your gender nor whether you have children nor marry. If you want to go to college and have a career, I support you."* You were blessed to have a mother who always supported your calling to lead. When she retired from her own profession, she passed down her special items she had acquired to adorn her office during her career. These items symbolized her desire for you to stay the course toward your calling to lead. These items remain on display in your office to this day.

In the South, Black girls from working-class backgrounds had three career choices: marry, become a maid, or teach.[155] It took you a long time to understand your calling and purpose in life. While you began your career as a housekeeper, you "uplifted" yourself to a much greater calling.

Today, young women of color are leading Fortune 500 companies and own their own businesses. Although you did not lead a Fortune 500 company, you did lead the equivalent of a mid-size company comprised of 205 employees in higher education.

In some respects, it was a revelation for you to finally acknowledge later in life— comfortably independent, unmarried, and childfree—that your lifestyle did not fit societal norms for women. That was okay. Your mother's encouragement gave you the reassurance that it was okay to live a life outside of societal norms. Peggy McIntosh's article on "White Privilege" provided further evidence that these privileges enabled a framework to exist for Whites to continue their dominance and oppression of marginalized groups. The author asserted that her "skin color was an asset for any move that she was educated to want to make" and suggested that "established and socially embedded privileges have enabled white people and males to define how women or people of color may perceive something as racism or sexism through their control of power and knowledge." McIntosh suggested, "Unless majority whites or males defined something as racism or sexism, existence of these oppressions is denied; white people and males control the definitions and identification of racism and sexism in western culture."[156]

In 2002, Charisse Jones and Kumea Shorter-Goodsen conducted a first-of-its kind research study called the "African American Women's Voices Project."[157] The focus of the study was to interview Black women in all sectors of their lives from various working environments throughout the country to find out their experiences in environments with race and gender diversity. The purpose was to "learn about African Americans' experiences of racial and gender stereotypes, bias and discrimination to understand what it felt like; and how they reacted and responded to it. They wanted to know about the impact of racism and sexism on the different aspects of these women's lives."[158] The study revealed that racist and sexist attitudes and discriminatory behavior was still taking a significant toll on Black women.

1. Race discrimination against Black women persists. Of the women surveyed, 90 percent said they had experienced discrimination, and 10 percent had been called the "Niggar" word in their lives.
2. Gender discrimination against Black Women was also pervasive. Of the women, 60 percent reported that they had experienced bias or discrimination based on gender.
3. Most Black women "shift" their behavior to accommodate others. Of the surveyed, 58 percent indicated that at times they changed the way they acted to fit in or be accepted by White people. A full 79 percent said that to gain acceptance, they have changed the way they speak, toned down their

mannerisms, talked about what they felt White people were interested in, and avoided controversial topics.

4. Discrimination was experienced most frequently at work. While Black women responded to racism and sexism in various arenas, it was in the workplace that they encountered it most often. Of the women, 69 percent said that they had experienced racial or gender discrimination at work. Issues related to the workplace, including getting hired, being paid equitably, and being promoted fairly, emerged as the major difficulties they experienced.

5. Black women frequently submerged their talents and strengths to support Black men. Of the women surveyed, 45 percent had at times down played their abilities or strengths with Black men.[159]

These findings support some of the experiences you have shared in your stories working in PWIs as well as what has been shared by other women leading in the academy. The coping strategies described in the Voices Project resonated with some of the strategies you have practiced to sustain your leadership as well, such as the previously mentioned:

> Speaking one way in the office, another way to your
> friends, and family; working overtime when you
> are exhausted to prove you are not lazy, learning
> how to ignore a comment you believe is racist or to
> address it in such as way that the person who said
> it does not label you threatening or aggressive; over
> preparing for a course to prove that you are just as
> capable as your peers who have more social capital
> than you do, keeping a positive attitude about
> yourself regardless what society projects you to be,
> or finding the need to fight back.[160]

Your ability to "shift" and adjust in a working environment/ profession which historically has not embraced women like you, is a call for you to include your voice in scholarly literature. Now that you are an executive leader, you have been instrumental in bringing empathy for the employee into the workplaces you have led. Times have changed for the better, but there is more work to be done.

In the book *Leading Coherently: Reflections from Leaders Around the World,* the authors suggested, "Congruent behavior both reflects and reinforces core values with a coherent relationship between leadership formation and performance."[161] The core values that were modeled by your parents reinforced the "gold collar" work ethic that you exhibit every day through integrity, transparent communication, accountability, respecting others, and excellence.[162] Your early childhood experiences provided you with an awareness that has helped to shape the adult that you are today.

Today, you lead one of the largest diverse departments on the UVM campus. Throughout your career, you have led by coaching employees on how to work together to achieve common goals. You have modeled the way for them to treat each other the way they would like to be treated within the parameters of the institution's guidelines, often referred to as the "platinum rule," which embraces the concept of Womanism. You accomplished this by using transparent communications, collaboration, effective interpersonal skills, respecting and empowering your employees, meeting the employee in their space at their level, providing a safe space where your employees have a voice, coaching and mentoring your direct reports, and being an accessible leader. The lessons learned from your experience with poor leadership models throughout your trajectory helped to shape the leader you have become. Over time, your leadership style modeling servant, collaborative, and transformational leadership traits emerged.

The institution recruited you for your current position based upon your human capital and experience as a change agent who demonstrated experience leading a diverse staff. In your current role, you lead a department of 205 employees, consisting of 20 different ethnic groups, some of the lowest-paid employees on your campus who are represented by the United Workers of America. UVM embodied the kind of employer characteristics that you had been searching for in your career at that time. It was the right place at the right time in your professional career to be able to give back to the group of employees who needed you the most.

In 2007, you returned to your first love, working with the most marginalized population in the facilities profession, the housekeepers. Having grown from a housekeeper early in your career to a director, you could not only talk the talk, but you could walk the walk. You had instant credibility with the housekeepers because you had been one. In this role, you are the voice for the department. Who better to advocate on behalf of the housekeepers than someone who they can identify with to look after their interests? Experience has taught you that building trust with your staff is a must if you are going to be an effective leader. As stated in the reading, trust takes time to build and can be destroyed in a moment.[163] Being straightforward comes easy when you have earned the respect of your staff. You modeled a "gladvocacy" communication strategy when it came to social justice issues involving your staff. The term "gladvocacy" is one of the five social justice communication strategies of Robert Nash: "A gladvocate teaches through invitation, generosity, and setting an example of tenuous tenacity."[164] You have used teachable moments to educate the dominant group how to treat you. It has been your experience working with social justice issues that "unresolved conflict can shut down communication, the key to social justice advocacy."[165] You believe out of all of the traits a leader can have, the single most important trait is integrity. You were called to do this work; you do not see it as just a job, but as a way of life. You approach your calling with humility and passion.

How have you sustained your leadership performance? It has been your experience that organizations rise as high as their leadership. As previously mentioned: if the leadership is poor, the organization will perform poorly; if the leadership performance is high, the organization will excel. An effective leader must have a vision, direction, and plan on how to proceed to get there. You have demonstrated repeatedly through various change initiatives that you are such a leader.

You have worked very hard to promote employees based upon competencies such as education, knowledge, skills, and work experience. As a leader, you have found creating a shared vision, mission, and core value statement with the leaders in your department helps in fostering inclusion and understanding of the department's mission in the absence of clear directive. You have found that it helps to give the staff a sense of pride and empowerment that their roles are important to the institution. Through your leadership, you have created a set of core values with the acronym "I CARE" (integrity, communication, accountability, respect, and excellence). Your department's vision is in line with the institutional vision and mission. Stemming from the shared vision has been the shared development of strategic goals to set the vision into a planned course of action.

You have always believed that a good leader develops their staff. Leaders need to be able to set an example for their managers and staff to emulate. As a leader, you have mentored staff members who have potential, the ones who stand above the rest in performance. You have worked with their strengths and given them the tools they need to become successful leaders. You have established resources for employees to gain the skills and education they need to develop competencies so that they can excel in their careers. A good leader plans to leave their organization in a better place than it was when they acquired it. They help to shape the vision, and they motivate and empower staff to reach it. They make the hard decisions when necessary, and they continuously seek new and innovative ways to make change and achieve continuous improvement. You encourage your staff members to think outside the box and to view challenges as opportunities.

Throughout most of your career, you have worked with staff members who are stationed at the bottom of the economic scale; as a result, your staffers have oftentimes brought their HOME life with them to work. You establish work life support systems on the job to support these employees to improve their quality of life on and off the job.

Finding your purpose in life has been a journey—not a destination. In 2007, you fulfilled another calling. You applied to the UVM EDLP program, upon which you were accepted. The course content addressed controversial real-world issues that were not viewed through rose-colored lenses. You are passionate about leadership and the role that has evolved for women and women of color in higher education; you have a lot to offer society at large and a lot to learn. This doctoral program helped you to find your voice as a woman, a person of color, and a leader.

As Roland Smith Jr. wrote:

> Whatever small contributions attributed to me by those whose lives I have touched are the contributions of countless ancestors who survived crucibles far more horrific, or exhilarating, than any of us today can imagine! Recounting my crucibles reminds me that our charge as mentors is to accept proudly the baton from our ancestors, do our part with honor as long as we are able, and pass the baton confidently to the next generation of educational leaders and mentors.[166]

While President Obama opened the door of possibilities for people of color, your dream is to ensure that the door remains open by contributing to the growing body of scholarly research on women of color and to leave a legacy for those to follow. As Angela Humphrey Brown wrote:

> Historically, the burden of racial uplift has been placed on the shoulders of all educated African Americans. Still, the primary uplifters of the race were African-American women, and so much so as suggested by Perkins and cited in Brown, the term "racial uplift" was synonymous with African-American women. African women were seen as the nurturers of race, and to that end they have been responsible for helping others in their families and communities achieve and appreciate their lots in life and in history.[167]

I believe only then will you have fulfilled your purpose and achieved the American dream.
Best wishes,
Leslye

Conclusion

> *The Pains of our past cannot be released until*
> *We touch them with healing and forgiveness.*
> *The truth about our childhood is stored Up in our body, and*
> *although we can repress it, We can never alter it.*
> *Our intellect can be deceived,*
> *Our feelings manipulated,*
> *Our conceptions confused,*
> *And our body tricked with medication,*
> *But someday our body will present its bill,*
> *For it is as incorruptible as a child who,*
> *Still whole in spirit;*
> *Will accept no compromise or excuse,*
> *And it will not stop tormenting us until*
> *We stop evading the truth.*[168]
>
> —Alice Miller, age 32

When I read that poem the first time, it moved me to tears because it exemplified all of the baggage I had carried into adulthood with me: the divorce of my parents at a young age, the impact of being a military brat, frequent relocations and learning to adapt in different spaces, the physical damage of 26 years of smoking and the successful quit, overcoming racial and sexual harassment, a lack of mentors and poor examples of leadership, and a lack of social capital. Once I understood my purpose in life and that I was called to lead and advocate for people of color, I promised myself that I would complete my terminal degree, and I found my scholarly voice along the way. I released the hurt from my past to open up the promise of my future.

Chapter Six: Implications: Dr. Kornegay's Recommendations to PWIs

SPN writing is all about the use of universal themes.
—Robert Nash

"So What?"

While the representation of Black women leading in PWIs has become a reality, I do not believe the dream has been fully realized. Higher Education, especially PWIs, still has a lot of work to do in the areas of recruitment, retention, and mentoring of women who lead or aspire to lead in the academy.

I believe the themes that emerged in my own narrative are applicable to the experiences of other Black women working in leadership roles in academia. I have learned how to do environmental scans whenever I find myself in a new location to assess the political landscape and organizational climate before diving into my role, to pick my battles and to be strategic in how I resolve challenges, and to build alliances and networks so that I am better able to cope with and navigate challenges that might come my way. I have learned the further I ascend into leadership, the more vulnerable I am as a Black woman working in PWIs. During times when my leadership was challenged, the support networks that should have been in place for women like me did not exist or were compromised. Is there any wonder why the retention rate for Black women leading in PWIs is low? I know now there is nothing wrong with practicing self-efficacy; I have learned if you do not speak up for yourself no one else will.

"Now What?"

The recurring theme of implications for Black women leading or aspiring to lead in PWIs suggests a need for higher education to review its role as the institutions that help to mold and shape our future generations. Evangelina Holvino, in her article "Diversity, Organizational Change, and Working with Differences: What Next?" talked about an experience she had during a workshop in Ghana. In the article, she shared how she "had been invited to the workshop to share her organization's [Center for Gender in Organizations] approach to gender and institutional change, and its potential application in universities in Africa with gender representative of six such universities." She learned many of the African nations' policies were supportive of African women's rights. Additionally, those nations provided a more supportive landscape for institutional change in higher education than the diminishing affirmative action policies in the United States. She shared how the workshop participants she was involved with "generated a vision of an equitable, diverse, and inclusive university that was one of the most encompassing visions she had ever seen in her 20 years of diversity work." The vision consisted of "mission, student-staff-faculty relations, curriculum, physical safety, and representation of diverse groups across different hierarchical levels."[169]

Moreover, Holvino suggested:

> The biggest mistake we make in diversity work
> is failing to pay attention to the context in which
> diversity work happens and how that context
> shapes some of the opportunities as well as the
> dilemmas and challenges faced.[170]

According to Holvino, to change this, it's important to "pay attention to the historical, social-political, economic, cultural, and organizational context of any diversity effort we may be involved in."[171] For this to happen, I believe PWIs need to establish policies and practices that truly reflect and support the organization's commitment to diversity (equity is inclusive of diversity) and inclusion across all levels.

The vision described by Holvino is an excellent model for PWIs in higher education to aspire to model themselves after. Black women must be a part of this vision and at the table working to make this change happen. I submit that in order for this to become reality, PWIs must make a shift in the recruitment and retention of Black women as well as provide formal mentoring and sponsoring opportunities to support Black women in the academy as students, leaders, and faculty.

The vision is only the beginning of what needs to happen for successful change to take shape in PWIs. Holvino took it a step further by suggesting:

> What makes for success seems to be a complex combination of factors, including leadership commitment, internal constituencies for change, pressure from outside, and a good business case as starters for organizational change success.[172]

The study "Best Practices in Achieving Workforce Diversity" was conducted by the US Department of Commerce and former Vice President Al Gore for the National Partnership for Reinventing Government Benchmarking study. It resulted in the following findings: "organizations benefit from diversity, leaders and managers are responsible for diversity, leaders and managers must create a strategic plan to develop diversity initiatives through the organization, and employees' views and involvement are key to the success of diversity initiatives."[173]

The authors of the study also emphasized that:

> Leaders and employees should take active roles in implementing these diversity processes, which in order to succeed should be fully aligned to core organizational goals and objectives. The benefits of diversity are for everyone. Diversity is more than a moral imperative; it is a global necessity. Moreover, diversity is an essential component of any civil society.[174]

While I agree with most of the study's findings, I wonder why women like me continue to be underrepresented in PWIs.

Although many PWIs have diversity plans collecting dust someplace or they are creating one, I challenge them to put those plans into action. Our student population is changing; we know already that the ethnic and racial populations will exceed the dominant group entering into our institutions around 2025. I want to encourage higher education institutions to think about what this will look like for their organization. I want to ask them: Are you prepared for the students of the future? Do you have leaders and faculty who represent underrepresented groups? If the answer is "no" to any of these questions, what do you plan to do to change?

"What Now" for Me?

As the leader of one of the largest diverse departments at UVM, I realized upon accepting the role that I would be the voice and advocate for my employees. I committed to this work and have actively served on a number of senior level committees since my arrival in 2007. I was commissioned to serve on the President's Commission for Race and Diversity for the university, I chaired the Diversity subcommittee, and I chaired the division's Diversity and Inclusion Committee for Enterprise and Finance Services. In addition, I served as a member of the Black Board Jungle Symposium planning committee, which held annual Educational Conferences for Faculty and Staff around diversity and inclusion for the university. The university made very aggressive efforts as well as adding a new Chief Diversity Officer. Reflecting back, there is more evidence that UVM was committed to doing the work that needed to be done, but they were not fully there yet. I believe implementing the recommendations made in this manuscript will require a change in the organizational climate for real change to take place.

In 2011, I was awarded the Master of Registered Environmental Sciences Executive, the highest designation in my profession. The credentials read:

> These credentials were designed to raise awareness of the knowledge, professionalism, and skill levels achieved by designation holders and to highlight their premier role as leaders and educators within IEHA and the housekeeping field. Just as a master's degree is an academic recognition granted to persons that have undergone a course of study showing mastery of a specific field of professional practice or study, IEHA's Master's Program will be for IEHA's elite members committed to continuous improvement and propagating professionalism.[175]

This recognition brought things full circle for me because I was honored as an expert and leader in a profession that I felt had failed to recognize my potential for more than 30 years. In 2009, I was profiled by the same organization's magazine. I was asked to give some advice or words of wisdom to others working in my profession that would benefit them as leaders. The editor called them "Leslye's Tips for Leadership." I want to add a few more tips to that list, based on what I have learned during my journey to leadership:

- Treat others the way they want to be treated within the parameters of the institution's policies and procedures.
- Be an ethical leader and lead with moral courage.
- A micromanaging leadership style is not leadership.
- Role model the leadership style you want others to emulate. You need to be able to talk the talk and walk the walk to have credibility among your team.
- Change should be embraced by everyone.
- Find that thing in your life that could help you better sustain your leadership, maintaining your health and wellness, such as meditation and confidence circles.
- Stay tuned into industry trends, such as new technology and best practices.
- Embrace continuous learning.
- Align yourself with positive people. Network and find a mentor and coach to help guide your professional development.
- Give back to your profession and your community by helping to lift up future leaders.
- Have faith in yourself and do not let anyone define for you what you can do.
- Practice transparent communication, collaboration, and inclusion.
- Establish a shared vision, mission, and core values with your team.

I believe that it is my purpose to lead and advocate for those less fortunate than myself and to be a voice for those who cannot be heard. The legacy I leave behind will be my leadership. As I think about all of the lessons that I have learned along the way, my practitioner experience of working with and leading underrepresented populations will be a valued asset in serving the changing demographics of the academy. My vision for my professional journey continues to be to advance beyond my current executive leadership role within PWI's. As I continue on in my journey, I will expand in knowledge, understanding, and wisdom in my daily leadership walk, and I wish you well on yours.

Letter to Higher Education/PWIs

Dear Higher Education/PWIs:

My mother could never protect me completely from you because your tentacles of racism, genderism, classism, and sexism expanded beyond her protective barrier—some subtle, others not so subtle. This behavior has been ingrained in the walls that bind you as an institution; it is ingrained in our society's culture. It is not surprising that we would find it in the very halls that should serve to educate our most precious gift to humankind—our children and future leaders.

Even though there have been a number of laws passed to ensure women like me are protected in the workplace, the literature suggests your institution's practices have not caught up to the policies and procedures you have on the books to address discrimination and diversity and inclusion concerns.

As Evangelina Holvino wrote, "We need better theory and practice to tackle some of the paradoxes that the discourse of diversity in this country has generated." She went on to suggest:

> At its best, the concept of diversity is based on the discriminatory effects that come to members of stigmatized groups because they belong to those groups, the concept is not based on individual differences, but rather group-level differences that provide advantages to some and disadvantages to others. But, in the effort to include all persons in diversity efforts, even those who are privileged by their group membership, diversity has come to mean any kind of "difference." In an increasingly conservative climate, individual differences

are preferred to group-focus explanations of inequality.[176]

Additionally, Holvino suggested:

We need to address the power of deeply-held beliefs such as individualism and meritocracy, which hinder understanding of the subtle and not-so subtle dynamics that create inequality in organizations. By meritocracy, I mean the belief that talent and hard work is all that is required to advance in an organization. It is difficult to convince others that "she did not make it" because of gender and racial discrimination when the prevalent assumptions are that "organizations are neutral, not gendered," "cream rises to the top," "you have to pay your dues," and "if you can't hack it you are not good for us anyway."[177]

It has been my experience that the very policies and procedures you created as a result of laws like the Civil Rights Act of 1968 and 1991 and the women's rights laws of 1974 have failed to support the very people that need them the most, Black women. White women have been the greatest benefactors of affirmative action, as evidenced by the Bureau of Labor Statistics.

Bibliography

ABC News, FULL TRANSCRIPT: Sen. Barack Obama's Victory Speech, November 4, 2008. http://abcnews.go.com/Politics/Vote2008/story?id=6181477&page=4#.Tw- obhxcL7Y.
Alpha Kappa Alpha Sorority, Incorporated. Last modified November 12, 2011. http://www.akal908.com.

American Council on Education, Center for Policy Studies, *The American College President*. Washington, DC, 2007.

Andelin, Helen. *The Fascinating Woman*. (Bantam, Updated edition, January 1, 1992).

Anyon, J. "Social Class and the Hidden Curriculum of Work," *Journal of Education* 162, no. 1: 67-92, edited by J. Ballantine, 257-278. (Mountain View, CA: Mayfield Publishing, 1989).

McGee Banks, Cynthia A, "Gender and Race as Factors in Educational Leadership and Administration." *The Jossey-Bass Reader on Educational Leadership,* 2nd ed., edited by J. Murphy, 229-338. (San Francisco: John Wiley & Sons, 2007).

Barksdale, Sydney H., "The Untold Story: African American Women Administrators' Alchemy of Turning Adversity Into Gold," Forum on Public Policy: 2007.

Beerel, Annabel. "How the Power Dynamics and the Culture of Fear in Business Organizations Contribute to the Gap Between Ethics and Morality in Business Practice." Ph.D. dissertation, Abstracts International. Section A: Humanities and Social Sciences, 2006, 64 no., 949.

Berry, Christian L., "Reconciling Contradictions: A Non-Traditional Perspective on Navigating the Academy." Master's Thesis, UVM, 2010.

Best Practices in Achieving Workforce Diversity, Executive Summary, U.S. Department of Commerce and Vice President Al Gore's National Partnership for Reinventing Government Benchmarking study.

Bordas, Juana, "How Salsa, Soul, and Spirit Strengthen Leadership," *Leader to Leader* 46, 2007.

Bordas, Juana, "Power and Passion: Finding Personal Purpose," *Reflections on Leadership* edited by L. S. Spears, 179-193. (New York: Wiley & Sons Inc., 1995).

Boyatzis, Richard and Annie McKee, *Resonant Leadership.* (Boston, MA: Harvard Business School Press, 2005).

Boyd, Melba Joyce, "Disappearing Acts: Black Face and the Tyranny of Intellectual Imperialism," *Our Stories II: The Experiences of Black Professionals on Predominantly White Campuses,* edited by Sherwood Smith and Mordean Taylor-Archer, 142-157. (Cincinnati, OH: The John D. O'Bryant Think Tank for Black Professionals in Higher Education on Predominantly White Campuses, 2006).

Bradley, DeMethra, "Outside Second-Generation, Inside First-Generation: Shedding Light on a Hidden Population in Higher Education," Ed.D. dissertation proposal, The University of Vermont, 2009.

Brown, Angela Humphrey, "African American Women of Inspiration," *Making Space,* edited by Vanessa Sheared and Peggy A. Sissel, (Westport, CT: Bergin & Garvey, 2001).

Bunker, Kerry A., "Leading in Times of Transition 12 Leader Competencies: What It Takes In Times of Transition," 2011, adapted from *CCL Publication Leading with Authenticity in Times of Transition as cited in Leading Effectively* e-Newsletter, October 2005.

Cherniss, Cary, "Leadership and Emotional Intelligence," *Inspiring Leaders,* edited by R. J. Burke and C. L. Cooper. (London: Routledge, 2006).

Collins, Patricia H., "Learning from Outsider Within: The Sociological Significance of Black Feminist Thought." *Social Problems,* volume 33, number 6, *Special Theory Issue,* Oct.-Dec. Sl4-S32. University of California Press on behalf of the Society for the Study of Social Problems, 1986.

Collins, Patricia Hill, *Black Feminist Thought: Knowledge, Consciousness, and the Politics of Empowerment,* (New York: Routledge, Chapman and Hall, Inc, 1991).

Covey, Stephen R., *Principle-Centered Leadership.* (Simon & Schuster, 1990).

Crawford, Kijana and Danielle Smith, "The We and the Us: Mentoring African-American Women," *Journal of Black Studies* 36(1): September 2005.

Creswell, John W., *Research Design: Qualitative, Quantitative, and Mix Methods Approaches,* 3rd ed. (Los Angeles: Sage, 2009).

Creswell, John W., *Qualitative Inquiry & Research Design: Choosing Among Five Approaches,* (Thousand Oaks, CA: Sage Publications, 2007).

Cropper, Beverly A., and Philomena Harrison, *Real or Imagined-Black Women's Experiences in the Academy, Community, Work & Family,* 3(2), 2000.

Diaz, Jacob L., "Marginalized Narratives in the Academy: One Chicano's Story Of His Journey in Higher Education," Ed.D. dissertation proposal. The University of Vermont, 2004.

Dumais, S., "Cultural Capital, Gender, and School Success: The Role of Habitus." *Sociology of Education* 75: 2002.

Economy, Peter, and Bob Nelson, *Managing for Dummies,* 3rd Ed. (Hobokin NJ: Wiley Incorporated, 2010).

Gaetane, J.M., "Black Women Administrators in Historically Black Institutions: Social Justice Project Rooted in Community. *Journal of Women in Educational Leadership,* 2(1): 2004.

Harvey, W.B., "Introduction: The Climb to the Top," *Grass Roots and Glass Ceilings: African-American Administrators in Predominantly White Colleges and Universities.* (New York, NY: State University of New York Press, 1999).

Harvey, William B., Eugene L. Anderson, Minorities in Higher Education: Twenty-First Annual Status Report. 2003-2004, (Washington DC: American Council on Education. February 2005).

Heading Grant, Wanda, and Judith A. Aiken, "Cross-Cultural Mentoring Relationships: A Recipe for Success," *Women of Color in Leadership Taking Their Rightful Place,* edited by Richard G. Johnson and G. L. A. Harris, 43-64. (San Diego, CA: Birkdale Publishers, 2010).

Holvino, Evangelina, "Diversity, Organizational Change, and Working with Differences: What Next?" *Beyond Diversity.-*

Working Across Differences for Organizational Change. Center for Gender Organization Commentaries, 3: June 2005.

hooks, bell, *Feminist Theory: From Margin to Center,* 2nd edition, (Cambridge, MA: South End Press Classics, 2000).

hooks, bell, *Ain't I a Woman.* (Boston, MA: South End Press, 1981).

Hunter, M. L., "If You're Light You're Alright: Light Skin Color as Social Capital for Women of Color," *Gender & Society* 16, 2: 2002.

Hurdle, Terri, "From Disappointment to Purpose: The Experiences of a Black Professional on a Predominantly White Campus," *Our Stories II: The Experiences of Black Professionals on Predominantly White Campuses,* edited by Sherwood Smith and Mordean Taylor-Archer, 21-29. (Cincinnati, OH: The John D. O'Bryant Think Tank for Black Professionals in Higher Education on Predominantly White Campuses, 2006).

International Housekeepers Association. Last modified on November 12, 2011. http://www.ieha.org.

Jinkins, Deborah and Michael Jinkins, *The Character of Leadership: Political Realism and Public Virtue in Nonprofit Organizations,* (San Francisco: Jossey Bass Publications, 1998).

Johnson, Richard. G., III, and G.L.A. Harris, *Women of Color in Leadership: Taking Their Rightful Place.* (United States: Birkdale Publishers Inc., 2010).

Jones, Charisse, and Kumea Shorter-Gooden, *Shifting: The Double Lives of Black Women in America,* (New York: Harper and Collins, 2003).

Kornegay, Leslye R., "How Do Women in Senior Leadership Roles at UVM Employ Ethical Leadership When Managing Workplace Dilemmas?" Research pilot study, The University of Vermont, 2009.

Kornegay, Leslye R., "Leading with Moral Courage at a Research I, Public Ivy University: An African-American Woman's Journey from Custodian, to Custodial Director, to Doctoral Student," SPN Paper. The University of Vermont, 2009.

Kornfield, Jack, *The Art of Forgiveness, Loving Kindness, and Peace* (New York: Bantam Dell, 2002).

Lipmen-Blumen, Jay, *Connective Leadership: Managing in a Changing World,* (New York: Oxford Press, 2005).

Lopez, Isabel 0., "Becoming a Servant Leader: The Personal Purpose," *Reflections on Leadership,* edited by L. S. Spears, (New York: Wiley & Sons, Inc., 1995).

Lorde, Audre, *Sister Outsider: Essays and Speeches,* (Berkeley, CA: Crossing Press, 1984).

Lorde, Audre, and Cheryl Clarke, *Sister Outsider: Essays and Speeches,* (New Forward, Random House Digital, Inc., 2007).

Maitra, A., "An Analysis of Leadership Styles and Practices of University Women In Administrative Vice Presidencies," Ph.D. Dissertation, Bowling Green State University, 2007.

The Martin Luther King, Jr. Research and Education Institute, "I Have a Dream" (28 August 1963), last modified on November 27, 2011. http://mlkkppOl.stanford.edu/index.php/encyclopedia/encyclopedia/enc_i_have_a_dream_28_august_1963.

Maxwell, John, *Leadership Gold: Lessons I've Learned From a Lifetime of Leading.* (Nashville, TN: Thomas Nelson Publishers, 2008).

McGee Banks, Cynthia A., "Gender and Race as Factors in Educational Leadership and Administration," *The Jossey-Bass Reader on Educational Leadership,* 2nd edition, edited by J. Murphy (ed.), 229-338. (San Francisco: John Wiley & Sons, 2007).

McIntosh, Peggy, "White Privilege and Male Privilege: A Personal Account of Coming to See Correspondences Through Work in Women's Studies," *Race, Class, and Gender,* edited by M. L. Anderson and P.H. Collins, (Belmont, CA: Wadsworth Pub., 1998).

McLeod, Jay, *Ain't No Makin It,* (Boulder, CO: Westview Press, 1995).

McWhorter, J. H., "Explaining the Black Education Gap." *WQ* (Wilson Quarterly), Summer 2000, 72-92.

Miller, Fayneese S., "Untangling the Ivy Vines," *Women of Color in Leadership Taking Their Rightful Place,* edited by Richard G. Johnson and G. L.A. Harris, (San Diego, CA: Birkdale Publishers, 2010).

Mosley, Juliana M., "Just Do it: Navigating the Doctoral Process," *Our Stories II: The Experiences of Black Professionals on Predominantly White Campuses,* edited by Sherwood Smith and Mordean Taylor-Archer. (Cincinnati, OH: The John D. O'Bryant Think Tank for Black Professionals in Higher Education on Predominantly White Campuses, 2006).

Nash, Robert J., and DeMethra L. Bradley, *Me-Search and Re-Search: A Guide for Writing Scholarly Personal Narrative Manuscripts,* (Charlotte, NC: Information Age Publishing Inc., 2011).

Nash, Robert J., *Liberating Scholarly Writing: The Power of Personal Narrative,* (New York: Teachers College Press, 2004).

Nash, Robert, "What Is the Best Way to Be a Social Justice Advocate? Communication Strategies for Effective Social Justice Advocacy," *About Campus,* May-June 2010.

Obama, Barack. "Senator Barack Obama's Victory Speech: Senator Barack Obama Delivers Victory Speech from Grant Park in Chicago." Last modified November 4, 2008. http://abcnews.go.com/print?id=6181477.

Parham-Payne, Wanda V. 2008. "Through the Lens of Black Women: The Significance of Obama's Campaign," *Journal of African American Studies, 2008.* Last modified December 16, 2008, 16, Springer Science+ Business Media, LLC.

Paz-Amor, Windy, "Courage Could Not Have Come at a Worst Time," Master's Thesis: *A Pluralistic Approach to Addressing Sexual and Gender Based Violence on College Campuses,* May 2010.

Pipher, Mary, *Writing to Change the World,* (New York: Penguin Group, 2006).

Pritchard, Ray, *Frequently Asked Questions about the Christian Life,* (B&H Publishing Group, 2001).

Samier, E., "The Problem of Passive Evil in Educational Administration: Moral Implications of Doing Nothing," *International Studies in Educational Administration (Commonwealth Council for Educational Administration & Management (CCEAM)),* March 2008, 36(1).

Sheared, Vanessa, and Peggy A. Sissel, foreword by Phyllis M. Cunningham, (Pub., Bergin, and Garvey, 2001) "Making Space, Merging Theory and Practice in Adult Education, bell hooks as cited in Sue Shore, *Talking about Whiteness: Adult Learning Practices and the Invisible Norms."*

Singham, M., "The Achievement Gap: Myths and Realities." *Phi Delta Kappan,* April 2023.

Smith, Roland B., "Muses of a Mentor: A Tribute to the Elders," *Our Stories II: The Experiences of Black Professionals on Predominantly White Campuses,* edited by Sherwood Smith and Mordean Taylor-Archer, 21-29, (Cincinnati, OH: The John D. O'Bryant Think Tank for Black Professionals in Higher Education on Predominantly White Campuses, 2006).

Smith, Sherwood, and Mordean Taylor-Archer, *Our Stories II: The Experiences of Black Professionals on Predominantly White Campuses,* (Cincinnati OH: The John D. O'Bryant Think Tank for Black Professionals in Higher Education on Predominantly White Campuses, 2006).

Spears, L.C., "Servant Leadership and the Greenleaf Legacy," *Reflections on Leadership,* edited by L.C. Spears, (New York: John Wiley Publishers, 1995).

Stanford-Blair, N., and M. H. Dickmann, *Leading Coherently: Reflections from Leaders Around the World,* (Thousand Oaks, CA: Sage Publications, 2005).

Stockett, Kathryn, *The Help,* (Amy Einhorn Books & Putnam, 2009).

Sturdivant, Alvin A., "On My Journey Now: An African American Search For Direction, Definition and Destiny in the Academy," Ed.D. dissertation proposal, The University of Vermont, 2007.

Trevino, Linda K., Laura P. Hatman, and Michel Brown, "Moral Person and Moral Manager: How Executives Develop a

Reputation for Ethical Leadership," *Contemporary Issues in Leadership,* 6th ed., edited by W. E. Rosenbach and R. L. Taylor, 2006.

The US Opportunities Commission. Last modified on October 10, 2011. http://www.eeoc.gov/laws/statutes/cra-1991.cfm.

Walker, Alice, *The Color Purple,* (New York: Washington Square Press, 1983).

Weston, Sherryl N., "The Phoenix Rising," *Our Stories II: The Experiences of Black Professionals on Predominantly White Campuses,* edited by Sherwood Smith and Mordean Taylor-Archer, (Cincinnati, OH: The John D. O'Bryant Think Tank for Black Professionals in Higher Education on Predominantly White Campuses, 2006).

Webster online dictionary: http://www.merriam-webster.com

Wikipedia: http://www.wikipedia.org

Endnotes

1. Martin Luther King Jr., "I Have a Dream" (28 August 1963).
2. Patricia Hill Collins, *Black Feminist Thought: Knowledge, Consciousness, and the Politics of Empowerment* (New York: Routledge, Chapman and Hall, Inc., 1991).
3. Helen Andelin, *The Fascinating Woman* (Bantam; Updated edition, January 1, 1992).
4. Collins, *Black Feminist*, page 5.
5. Audre Lorde, *Sister Outsider: Essays and Speeches* (Berkeley, CA: Crossing Press, 1984), page 112.
6. bell hooks, *Feminist Theory: From Margin to Center*, 2nd ed. (Cambridge, MA: South End Press Classics, 2000).
7. Collins, *Black Feminist*, pages 4-6.
8. Ibid., pages 5-6.
9. Ibid., pages 5-6.
10. Angela Humphrey Brown, "African American Women of Inspiration," *Making Space*, edited by Vanessa Sheared and Peggy A. Sissel, 2001, pages 214-226 (Westport, CT: Bergin & Garvey, 2001), pages 214-226.
11. Ibid., page 215.
12. Charisse Jones and Kumea Shorter-Gooden, *Shifting: The Double Lives of Black Women in America.* (New York: Harper and Collins, 2003), pages 5-6.
13. Ibid., page 5.
14. Cynthia A. McGee Banks, "Gender and Race as Factors in Educational Leadership and Administration," *The Jossey-Bass Reader on Educational Leadership, Second Edition,* (San Francisco: John Wiley & Sons, Inc., 2007), pages 299-338.
15. Collins, *Black Feminist*, page 12.
16. bell hooks, *Ain't I a Woman* (Boston, MA: South End Press, 1981), page 160.
17. Ibid., page 160.
18. Alice Walker, *The Color Purple* (New York: Washington Square Press, 1983).
19. Kathryn Stockett, *The Help* (Amy Einhorn Books & Putnam, 2009).
20. Jones and Shorter-Goodsen, *Shifting,* page 7.
21. Collins, *Black Feminist*, pages 37-38.
22. Ibid., page 38.
23. Ibid., page 38.
24. Alvin A. Sturdivant, "On My Journey Now: An African American Search for Direction, Definition, and Destiny in the Academy" (EdD dissertation proposal, The University of Vermont, 2007).

25. Jacob Diaz, "Marginalized Narratives in the Academy: One Chicano's Story of His Journey in Higher Education" (EdD dissertation proposal, The University of Vermont, 2004).

26. Ibid., "Marginalized."

27. Patricia H. Collins, "Learning from Outsider Within: The Sociological Significance of Black Feminist Thought," *Social Problems,* page 33, number 6, Special Theory Issue, October-December (1986): S14-S32. University of California Press on behalf of the Society for the Study of Social Problems.

28. DeMethra Bradley, "Outside Second-Generation, Inside First-Generation: Shedding Light on a Hidden Population in Higher Education," (EdD dissertation proposal, The University of Vermont, 2009).

29. Juliana M. Mosley, "Just Do it: Navigating the Doctoral Process," *Our Stories II: The Experiences of Black Professionals on Predominantly White Campuses,* edited by Sherwood Smith and Mordean Taylor-Archer, 2006, pages 74-82 (Cincinnati, OH: The John D. O'Bryant Think Tank for Black Professionals in Higher Education on Predominantly White Campuses).

30. Sherryl N. Weston, "The Phoenix Rising," *Our Stories II: The Experiences of Black Professionals on Predominantly White Campuses,* edited by Sherwood Smith and Mordean Taylor-Archer, 2006, pages 2-11 (Cincinnati, OH: The John D. O'Bryant Think Tank for Black Professionals in Higher Education on Predominantly White Campuses).

31. Ibid., pages 2-11.

32. Cynthia A. McGee Banks, *Gender and Race,* pages 229-338.

33. Leslye R. Kornegay, "Leading with Moral Courage at a Research I, Public Ivy University: An African-American Woman's Journey from Custodian, to Custodial Director, to Doctoral Student" (SPN Paper, The University of Vermont, 2009).

34. *The American College President.* (Washington, DC: American Council on Education, Center for Policy Studies, 2007).

35. Leslye Kornegay, "How Do Women in Senior Leadership Roles at UVM Employ Ethical Leadership when Managing Workplace Dilemmas?" (Research pilot study paper, The University of Vermont, 2009).

36. Robert J. Nash and DeMethra L. Bradley, *Me-Search in Re-Search: A Guide for Writing Scholarly Personal Narrative Manuscripts* (Information Age Publishing Inc, 2011), page 119.

37. Bradley, "Outside-Second-Generation."

38. Nash and Bradley, *Me-Search,* page 16.

39. John W. Creswell, *Qualitative Inquiry & Research Design: Choosing Among Five Approaches* (Thousand Oaks, CA: Sage Publications, 2007), pages 53-55.

40. Ibid., pages 53-55.
41. Nash and Bradley, *Me-Search*, page 16.
42. Ibid., page 16.
43. Ibid., page 16.
44. Ibid., page 84.
45. Ibid., page 17.
46. Ibid., page 18.
47. Wanda Heading-Grant and Judith A. Aiken, "Cross-Cultural Mentoring Relationships: A Recipe for Success," *Our Stories II: The Experiences of Black Professionals on Predominantly White Campuses,* edited by Sherwood Smith and Mordean Taylor-Archer, 2006, pages 43-64 (Cincinnati, OH: The John D. O'Bryant Think Tank for Black Professional in Higher Education on Predominantly White Campuses).
48. Nash and Bradley, *Me-Search,* page 19.
49. Ibid., page 19.
50. Ibid., pages 19-20.
51. John W. Creswell, *Research Design: Qualitative, Quantitative, and Mix Methods Approaches,* 3rd ed. (Los Angeles: Sage, 2009), page 13.
52. Nash and Bradley, *Me-Search*, page 84.
53. Bradley, "Outside Second-Generation."
54. Nash and Bradley, *Me-Search,* page 109.
55. Nash and Bradley, *Me-Search*, pages 110-111.
56. Ibid., page 111.
57. Christian L. Berry, "Reconciling Contradictions: A Non-Traditional Perspective on Navigating the Academy (Master's Thesis, The University of Vermont, May, 2010).
58. Nash and Bradley, *Me-Search,* pages 136-137.
59. Christine L. Berry, "Reconciling Contradictions," page 7.
60. Wikipedia, accessed October 9, 2011.
61. Maya Angelou, Volume Four of the Paris Review Interviews, 2009.
62. bell hooks, *Ain't I a Woman,* page 160.
63. Terri Hurdle, "From Disappointment to Purpose: The Experiences of Black Professionals on Predominantly White Campus," *Our Stories II: The Experiences of Black Professionals on Predominantly White Campuses,* edited by Sherwood Smith and Mordean Taylor-Archer, 2006, pages 43-45 (Cincinnati, OH: The John D. O'Bryant Think Tank for Black Professionals in Higher Education on Predominantly White Campuses).
64. bell hooks, *Ain't I a Woman.*
65. M. L Hunter, "If You're Light, You're Alright": Light Skin Color as Social Capital for Women of Color, *Gender & Society* 16:2 (2002 April) pages 175-193.
66. Ibid., pages 175-193.

67. J. H. McWhorter, "Explaining the Black Education Gap," *(WQ,* Wilson Quarterly, 2002 Summer) pages 72-92.
68. Chris Anyon, "Social Class," 1980.
69. Windy Paz-Amor, "Courage Could Not Have Come at a Worst Time: A Pluralistic Approach to Addressing Sexual- and Gender-Based Violence on College Campuses," (Alpha Kappa Alpha Sorority, Incorporated, May, 2010) pages 42-43.
70. M. Singham, "The Achievement Gap: Myths and Realities," *Phi Delta Kappan,* April, pages 586-591.
71. Saving and Loan Crisis, accessed online, November 12, 2011, http://en.wikipedia.org/wiki/Savings and loan crisis.
72. The US Opportunities Commission, accessed online October 10, 2011, http://www.eeoc.gov/laws/statutes/cra-l99l.cfm
73. Lorde, *Sisters Outsiders,* page 134.
74. Ibid., page 150.
75. Paz-Amor, *Courage,* pages 54-55.
76. Joseph Economy and Fonda Nelson, "Managing Leadership for Dummies," 3rd edition, *Wiley Incorporated,* Hobokin, NJ (2010), pages 28-30.
77. Lorde, *Sister Outsider,* page 112.
78. Frederick W. Taylor. "The Principles of Scientific Management" (New York: Harper & Row, 1911).
79. Lorde, *Sister Outsider,* page 174.
80. Jay McLeod, *Ain't No Makin It* (Boulder, CO: Westview Press, 1995).
81. Terri Hurdle, "From Disappointment to Purpose," *Our Stories II: The Experiences of Black Professionals on Predominantly White Campuses,* edited by Sherwood Smith and Mordean Taylor-Archer, 2006, pages 43-45 (Cincinnati, OH: The John D. O'Bryant Think Tank for Black Professionals in Higher Education on Predominantly White Campuses).
82. Boyd, "Disappearing Acts," page 154.
83. Nancy Stanford-Blair and Michael Dickmann, *Leading Coherently: Reflections from Leaders Around the World* (CA: Sage Publications, 2005).
84. Jay Lipmen-Blumen, *Connective Leadership: Managing in a Changing World* (New York: Oxford Press, 2005), pages 113-225.
85. Nancy Stanford-Blair and Michael Dickmann, *Leading Coherently,* page 67.
86. Linda K. Trevino, Laura P. Hatman, and Michel Brown, "Moral Person and Moral Manager: How Executives Develop a Reputation for Ethical Leadership," *Contemporary Issues in Leadership,* 6th edition, edited by W.E. Rosenbach and R. L. Taylor, (2006), pages 45-62.
87. Lipmen-Blumen, *Connective Leadership,* page 112.
88. Ibid., page 112.

89. Jones and Shorter-Goodsen, *Shifting,* page 7.
90. Robert Nash, "What Is the Best Way to be a Social Justice Advocate? Communication Strategies for Effective Social Justice Advocacy," *About Campus,* page 13.
91. Cary Cherniss, "Leadership and Emotional Intelligence," *Inspiring Leaders,* edited by R. J. Burke and C. L. Cooper (London: Routledge, 2006), pages 133-148.
92. Richard Boyatzis and Annie McKee, *Resonant Leadership* (Boston: Harvard Business School Press, 2005).
93. John Maxwell, *Leadership Gold: Lessons I've Learned from a Lifetime of Leading* (Nashville, TN: Thomas Nelson Publishers, 2008).
94. Stanford-Blair and Dickmann, *Leading Coherently,* page 131.
95. Stephen R. Covey, *Principle-Centered Leadership,* (Simon & Schuster, 1990).
96. Spears, "Servant Leadership and the Greenleaf Legacy," *Reflections on Leadership,* edited by L.C. Spears (New York: John Wiley Publishers, 1995), page 8.
97. A. Maitra, "An Analysis of Leadership Styles and Practices of University Women in Administrative Vice Presidencies" (PhD dissertation, Bowling Green State University, 2007).
98. J.M. Gaetane, "Black Women Administrators in Historically Black Institutions: Social Justice Project Rooted in Community," *Journal of Women in Educational Leadership,* volume 2 (1): pages 37-58.
99. Juana Bordas, "How Salsa, Soul, and Spirit Strengthen Leadership," *Leader to Leader,* volume 46 (2007): pages 35-41.
100. A. Beerel, "How the Power Dynamics and the Culture of Fear in Business Organizations Contribute to the Gap Between Ethics and Morality in Business Practice," (PhD dissertation, Abstracts International. Section A: Humanities and Social Sciences, 2006), page 64, number 949.
101. E. Samier, "The Problem of Passive Evil in Educational Administration: Moral Implications of Doing Nothing," *International Studies in Educational Administration (Commonwealth Council for Educational Administration & Management (CCEAM)),* 36(1): 2-21.
102. Ibid., page 19.
103. Bradley, "Outside First-Generation Inside Second-Generation," page 81.
104. Kerry A. Bunker and Michael Wakefield, Leading with Authenticity in Times of Transition (Centers for Creative Leadership, 2005).
105. Ibid., 2011.
106. Ibid., 2011.
107. Fayneese Miller, "Untangling the Ivy Vines," *Women of Color in Leadership Taking Their Rightful Place,* edited by Richard G.

Johnson and G. L. A. Harris (San Diego: Birkdale Publishers, 2010), pages 72-92.

108. Ibid., page 5.
109. Ibid., page 7.
110. Stephen Brookfield, personal communication, October, 20, 2011.
111. Beverley A. Cropper and Philomena Harrison, *Real or Imagined– Black Women's Experiences in the Academy, Community Work & Family*, 2000, 3(2).
112. Sidney H. Barksdale, "The Untold Story: African-American Women Administrators' Alchemy of Turning Adversity into Gold, *Forum on Public Policy* (2007).
113. Ibid., page 3.
114. Heading-Grant and Aiken, "Cross-Cultural Mentoring Relationships," page 44.
115. Ibid., page 45.
116. Ibid., page 47.
117. Ibid., page 47.
118. Ibid., page 59.
119. Kijana Crawford and Danielle Smith, "The We and the Us: Mentoring African-American Women," *Journal of Black Studies,* volume 36, number 1 (Sept., 2005), page 64.
120. Ibid., pages 64-67.
121. Vanessa Sheared and Peggy A. Sissel, foreword by Phyllis M. Cunningham, "Making Space, Merging Theory and Practice in Adult Education," (Bergin and Garvey, 2001), bell hooks as cited in Sue Shore, "Talking about Whiteness: Adult Learning Practices and the Invisible Norms," page 43.
122. Bureau of Labor Statistics (2010).
123. William B. Harvey and Eugene L. Anderson, "Minorities in Higher Education: Twenty-First Annual Status Report, 2003-2004," (Washington DC: American Council on Education, February 2005).
124. Collins, *Black Feminist,* page 12.
125. Ibid., page 12.
126. Ibid., page 12.
127. American Council on Education, Center for Policy Studies, *The American College President* (2007).
128. Jones and Shorter-Goodson, *Shifting,* pages 7-8.
129. Personal Communication, October 13, 2011.
130. Cherniss, "Leadership and Emotional Intelligence."
131. Mary Pipher, *Writing to Change the World.* (New York: Penguin Group), page 12.
132. Boyd, *Disappearing Acts,* page 143.
133. Ibid., page 143.

134. Deborah Jinkins and Michael Jinkins, *The Character of Leadership: Political Realism and Public Virtue in Nonprofit Organizations* (San Francisco: Jossey Bass Publications, 1998).
135. Jay MacLeod, *Ain't No Making It,* page 14.
136. Ibid., page 101.
137. Ibid., page 101.
138. S. Dumais, "Cultural Capital, Gender, and School Success: The Role of Habitus," *Sociology of Education* (2002), page 44.
139. Ibid., page 54.
140. Ibid., page 53.
141. MacLeod, *Ain't No Making It.*
142. Ibid., page 81.
143. Ibid., page 99.
144. Ibid., page 142.
145. Ibid., page 142.
146. Ibid., page 249.
147. Ibid., page 441.
148. Ibid., page 45.
149. Ibid., page 241.
150. Paz-Amor, "Courage Could Not Have Come at a Worst Time," page 17.
151. ABC News, FULL TRANSCRIPT: Sen. Barack Obama's Victory Speech, November 4, 2008. http://abcnews.go.com/Politics/Vote2008/story?id=6181477&page=4#.Tw obhxcL 7Y.
152. Audre Lorde and Cheryl Clarke, *Sister Outsider: Essays and Speeches,* (New Forward, Random House Digital, Inc., 2007), page 6.
153. Wanda V. Parham-Payne, "Through the Lens of Black Women: The Significance of Obama's Campaign," *Journal of African American Studies,* volume 13 (2009), pages 131-138.
154. Personal communication, November 8, 2008.
155. Brown, *African-American Women of Inspiration,* page 219.
156. Peggy McIntosh, "White Privilege and Male Privilege: A Personal Account of Coming to See Correspondences Through Work," *Women's Studies,* edited by M.L. Anderson and P.H. Collins, *Race, Class, and Gender* (Belmont, CA: Wadsworth Pub.), page 100.
157. Jones and Shorter-Goodsen, *Shifting,* page 8.
158. Ibid., page 4.
159. Ibid., pages 8-10.
160. Ibid., pages 7-8.
161. Stanford-Blair and Dickmann, *Leading Coherently,* page 112.
162. Ibid., page 141.
163. Ibid., page 67.
164. Nash, "What is the Best Way to be a Social Justice Advocate?" page 14.
165. Ibid., pages 1-14.

166. Roland Smith Jr., "Muses of a Mentor: A Tribute to the Elders," *Our Stories II: The Experiences of Black Professionals on Predominantly White Campuses,* edited by Sherwood Smith and Mordean Taylor-Archer, (Cincinnati, OH: The John D. O'Bryant Think Tank for Black Professionals in Higher Education on Predominantly White Campuses, 2006), page 29.

167. Brown, *African American Women of Inspiration*, page 220.

168. Jack Kornfield, *The Art of Forgiveness, Loving Kindness, and Peace.* (New York: Bantam Dell, 2002).

169. Evangelina Holvino, "Diversity, Organizational Change, and Working with Differences: What Next?" *Beyond Diversity: Working Across Differences for Organizational Change,* (Center for Gender Organization Commentaries, June 2004), page 1.

170. Ibid., page 1.

171. Ibid., page 1.

172. Ibid., page 3.

173. Best Practices in Achieving Workforce Diversity, Executive Summary, U.S. Department of Commerce and Vice President Al Gore's National Partnership for Reinventing Government Benchmarking study, pages 1-2.

174. Ibid., page 1.

175. IEHA Masters REH, accessed online: www.ieha.org, October 13, 2011.

176. Holvino, "Diversity, Organizational Change, and Working with Differences," pages 3-4.

177. Ibid., page 4.

Acknowledgments

"To whom much is given, much is required."

Luke 12:48

I want to thank everyone who has helped me to get to this place in my life. Without God in my life, it would not have been possible. I couldn't have done anything without Him in my life.

I also want to thank the *Sheroes* in my life.

To my mom, who we lost a couple of years after I did this work. My one great solace is that she lived to read it and attend my graduation.

And to my sister Fonda, you have always been there for me, and I am blessed to have you both in my life. While I have the support of all of my family, you two have been my biggest advocates. When it came time for me to leave *HOME* and move north to pursue my dream, you supported me during two relocations. Even though at times there was considerable distance between us, it is because of your strength and love that I was able to carry the image of *HOME* with me.

About the Author

Leslye Renee Kornegay, EdD, is currently serving in the role of Executive Director of University Facilities (UEVS) at Duke University. She resides in Durham, North Carolina.

In the thirteen years since her research was completed, a number of platforms have emerged that have given another voice for Black women across all professional genres to speak up about the "-ism's," work and life struggles, challenges, and barriers in the workplace. The rise of Facebook, Instagram, LinkedIn, X, Tik Tok, podcasts, YouTube, blogs, and private TV digital stations have opened up a wealth of Black women's experience.

Dr. Kornegay realizes that she was never alone in her experiences. Black women's voices were not as prevalent in the literature and social media as they are today—in both peer and non-peer contexts.

It is Dr. Kornegay's hope that her work can be used as a foundational piece for other Black women in their journeys. Although her focus and research have been on Black women in leadership, specifically in primarily white institutions (PWIs), she believes this book serves as a resource for nonwhites who work with Black women. It is also her hope this book serves as inspiration for Black women leaders in PWIs.